CREATIVE COSTUMES
FOR
CHILDREN
(Without Sewing)

Mark Walker

COOL HAND COMMUNICATIONS, INC.
A Publishing Company

Published by:
COOL HAND COMMUNICATIONS, INC.
1098 N.W. Boca Raton Boulevard
Suite #1
Boca Raton, FL 33432

Library of Congress #93-71984
ISBN: 1-56790-059-3

Printed in the United States of America

Photography by Laura Drogoul
Artwork by John Berndt

10 9 8 7 6 5 4 3 2 1
First Printing

For her unyielding patience and support,
I wish to thank my wife, Ginny.

ACKNOWLEDGMENTS

I would like to extend my deepest appreciation to the following individuals who helped me with this publication:

M O D E L S

Michael Hauser

Latosha Lovett

Elise Rosen

Alison Walker

Katie Walker

In addition, I would like to thank Laura Drogoul for her assistance with photography and make-up, and John Berndt of Baltimore Typography & Design for his illustrations.

TABLE OF CONTENTS

INTRODUCTION

In today's fast-paced society, many of us have forgotten about good old-fashioned skills. Years ago, for example, it was a necessity for a lot of men to know how to do simple car repairs or for many women to learn sewing. Today, that is no longer the case.

With sewing skills vanishing among the adult populace, the children of these parents are often left with several unpopular choices whenever they're looking for a costume for a masquerade, Halloween, school play, or other special event. The average costume house doesn't rent children's costumes, and the ones available are usually of a very low quality and expensive. Children's costume patterns are available from most fabric stores. But they are often too complicated for the average parent with just a slight sewing skill to master in the time left in his or her busy day.

Problems such as these are the reasons why this book was written. We have strived to keep all our patterns as simple as possible. All measurements are kept general, and precise measurements are never critical for the making of any costume. Given the materials, most costumes in this book can easily be done in an evening if not within a couple of hours. Every costume here was especially made for this publication and, to the best of our knowledge, is the first costume book that doesn't require sewing.

The reader may find parts of the text and illustrations somewhat repetitive. That's because it is our belief many people who are interested in this book are looking to make a particular costume. For their convenience, each costume is contained totally in its own section, and references to previous sections of text and illustrations are avoided.

MATERIALS, SOURCES AND GENERAL INFORMATION

 hroughout our book references are made to certain items that may be foreign to the novice costumer. We hope this list will save you valuable time when you need a certain product.

ALUMINUM WIRE: Most hardware stores carry this product.

CHEESECLOTH: Cheesecloth can be bought by the yard in any fabric shop.

CONTACT CEMENT: This strong adhesive glue can be found in most hardware stores. It is the perfect binding agent for foam rubber and anytime you wish to secure fabric to plastic. The ideal way to use this product is to coat two pieces of material with contact cement. When the glue has dried, press the two items together. Contact cement can also be applied to foam rubber to produce a skin-like coating which more readily takes paint than does untreated foam rubber.

MAKE-UP: Certain costumes in our book require make-up. Check your local phone book for a reliable costume shop or theatrical supplier nearest you.

PLASTIC TUBING: Tubing is available in most hardware stores.

POSTER BOARD: Art shops and stationary stores carry this product in different sizes and thicknesses. We use poster board for the construction of some novelty hats.

REED: This is a natural product found in craft shops. We use reed only for the making of the poppy costume, but don't be afraid to experiment with this product for other costumes using the same rules.

VINYL: This material can be found in most fabric shops. It comes in a variety of colors such as gold, silver and black.

WHITE GLUE: For most of our costumes we recommend you use white glue, such as Elmer's glue-all or Sobo, for adhesive purposes. A hot glue gun, however, works just as well. In some instances, hot glue is even preferred over white glue as it speeds up the normal drying process. But never iron any seams joined together with hot glue. It may damage your iron.

Happy New Year! It's time to ring out the old and bring in the new. And who better to represent the ending of the old year than Father Time himself.

MATERIALS NEEDED
* White fabric
* Sandals
* White crepe paper
* Painter's cap
* Rope
* White glue
* 2 Funnels, three 3/8-inch dowels, plywood, screw eye
(for hourglass)
* Duct tape
* Silver spray paint

Measure the distance from your child's shoulder to his feet. Whatever the measurement is, double it and add 12 inches to get the length of material you will need to make the robe. Next, have your child stand with his arms out from his sides like a scarecrow. Measure from wrist to wrist to get the width of material you will need to make the robe.

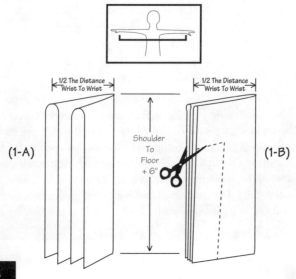

(1-A)

1/2 The Distance
Wrist To Wrist

Shoulder
To
Floor
+ 6"

1/2 The Distance
Wrist To Wrist

(1-B)

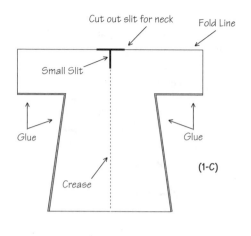

Cut out slit for neck

Fold Line

Small Slit

Glue

Glue

(1-C)

Crease

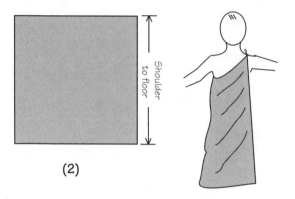

Shoulder to floor

(2)

Fold the material in half, first lengthwise and then again width-wise. (Illustration 1-A) Cut a piece out of the lower free corners as shown in illustration 1-B. Unfold the material widthwise revealing a bell-shaped pattern. (Illustration 1-C) Make an opening for the head by cutting a slit in the center lengthwise fold. Also make a slit down the center front crease. It is always best not to make the openings too big. Start small and increase it gradually until your child can fit his head in easily. Glue the side seams shut by applying white glue about 1/2 inch away from the edge of the fabric and then press the two pieces of material together with your fingers. When the glue has dried, turn the robe inside out to hide the seams. The robe is belted in at the waist with a cord. Blouse any excess length over the cord.

For the drape that hangs over the robe, take a piece of the same fabric used to make the robe and cut a large square, the sides of which should be the length of your child's shoulder-to-floor measurement. Taking two top corners, wrap the material around the body and tie the corners together over the left shoulder. (Illustration 2)

To make Father Time's wig and beard, use white crepe paper. Cut the paper in strips about 12 inches wide and 2 inches longer than the length that you want the wig and beard to be when finished. Now cut these strips vertically into 1-inch-wide strips leaving an uncut border at the top approximately 1 inch wide. (Illustration 3-A)

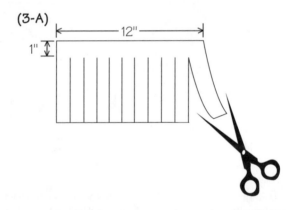

You can now curl the strips by holding one of the 1-inch strips between the thumb and first finger of the left hand just below the 1-inch border. Holding a pencil between the thumb and first finger of the right hand, place the paper strip between the thumb and the pencil. By gently pulling the pencil towards you and applying pressure on the pencil with the thumb you will cause the paper to curl. (Illustration 3-B) By applying more pressure with the thumb, the curl can be made tighter.

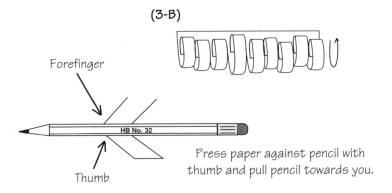

(3-B)

Forefinger

HB No. 32

Thumb

Press paper against pencil with thumb and pull pencil towards you.

Three strips of curls can now be glued together, one on top of the other at the 1-inch border. (Illustration 3-C) The bottom layer should have loose curls while the curls on each additional layer should become progressively tighter. These sets of curls may be attached to a painter's cap, which has had its brim removed, to form a wig. A piece of elastic or cloth tape can be attached to a set of curls to form the beard. This may be fastened under the chin and tied over the top of the head and under the hat.

(3-C)

Glue

Father Time is known for carrying two things: a scythe, for cutting away the old, and an hourglass that symbolizes time is passing on. If you are unable to find a plastic scythe at a novelty or costume shop, one can be made with a mop stick, some cardboard, masking tape and aluminum foil.

To make an hourglass, connect the spouts of two funnels with duct tape. (Two toilet plungers bolted together will also work.) To get the right shape, the spouts will probably need to be shortened. Cut two discs out of plywood that are about 1-1/2-inch larger in diameter than the wide end of the funnel. Lying the discs on top of each other, drill three 3/8-inch holes that tri-sect the circumference of the circle. (Illustration 4-A)

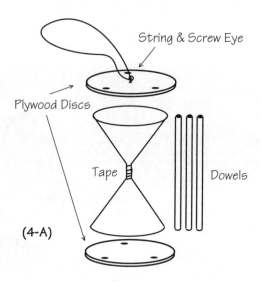

String & Screw Eye

Plywood Discs

Tape

Dowels

(4-A)

Hour Glass

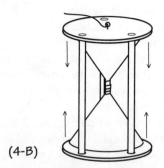

(4-B)

Connect the two pieces of wood together, sandwiching the funnels between, using the three dowels. The funnels and dowels can be held in place by glue. Put a screw eye in the top through which you thread a cord. (Illustration 4-B.) Make the cord long enough so that the hourglass can be hung around the neck. Spray paint it silver. To make the hourglass look more attractive add glitter to the funnels.

Cupid is the personification of love and romance.

MATERIALS NEEDED
* Pink leotard & tights
* Ballet slippers
* Gold metallic ribbon
* Soft white material (for tunic)
* Chiffon (pink or blue)
* A wig
* White glue
* Braided cord
* Red felt (for arrowhead)
* Wooden dowel (for arrow)
* 1-inch x 1/8-inch aluminum stock (for bow)

(1-A)

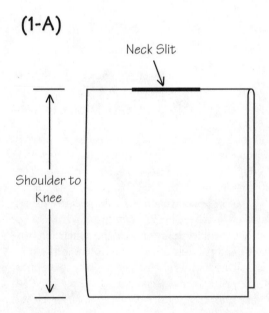

Neck Slit

Shoulder to Knee

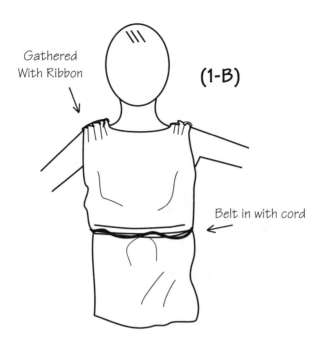

Gathered
With Ribbon

(1-B)

Belt in with cord

If by some chance your daughter is already enrolled in ballet classes, her cupid costume is 90% complete. Cupid's basic outfit consists of a pink leotard and tights and ballet slippers.

The tunic is essentially nothing more than a poncho that has been gathered at the shoulders with two pieces of ribbon tied through the neck hole. To make the tunic, take a piece of soft white material (the width should be wider than your child's shoulder-to-shoulder measurement and the length when folded in half should measure the same as that from your child's shoulder to knee). Fold the material in half lengthwise and put a slit in the center to put the head through. (Illustration 1-A) Next, simply take two ribbons or cords and gather the shoulders. Also take a cord and tie about the waist, and blouse the tunic up over the cord. (Illustration 1-B)

Use a pink or blue piece of chiffon to make a swag to go over the tunic. A swag is a piece of material that is draped diagonally across the chest and hangs on one shoulder. To drape the swag, safety pin one end on the right shoulder so that a bit of material hangs toward your child's back and the rest hangs down her front. Bring the long piece in the front around under her left arm and around her back and up over her right shoulder with a bit or so hanging toward the front. Pin in place.

To enhance the outfit, wrap gold metallic ribbon around the calves of each leg and tie in place. If available, use a yellow or blonde curly wig. A yellow clown wig will do the job; but if you can't locate one, spray paint a curly wig gold. When the wig is in place, tie another piece of gold metallic ribbon around the forehead to keep it secure.

Cupid's costume needs a bow and an arrow in order to be complete. To make the bow, use a piece of aluminum stock, about 1 inch by 1/8 inch, and bend it into the shape. (See illustration 2) Paint it gold and decorate with ribbons. Tie a piece of braided cord from one end of the bow to the other for the bow string. Use a wooden dowel to make Cupid's arrow. To make a heart-shaped tip, use white glue to attach two pieces of red felt to the dowel.

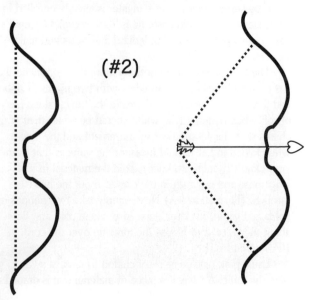

(#2)

A mischievous elf of Irish folklore, the leprechaun is the perfect costume to wear on Saint Patrick's Day.

MATERIALS NEEDED
* White long sleeved shirt
* Long white tube socks
* Green or white sweat pants
* Green felt
* Black material for tie
* White glue
* 1-inch masking tape
* Green spray paint
* Black ribbon or braid
* Wide black belt with a buckle
* Big buttons
* Black shoes
* Black felt
* Cardboard leprechaun hat

(1-A)

(1-B)

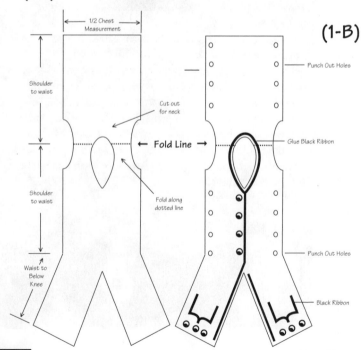

1/2 Chest Measurement

Shoulder to waist

Cut out for neck

Shoulder to waist

Fold along dotted line

Waist to Below Knee

← Fold Line →

Punch Out Holes

Glue Black Ribbon

Punch Out Holes

Black Ribbon

The leprechaun's vest is probably the most involved part of this costume, even though it is quite easy to make. Measure the distance from your child's shoulder to his waist. Whatever the measurement is, double it. Add that measurement to the measurement of your son's waist to just below his knee. This will be the length of material you will need to make the vest.

Following illustration 1-A, cut a vest out of green felt. Around the neck hole and down the center front, glue a piece of black ribbon or braid to give the vest added dimension. Also glue braid to create the illusion of pockets. For additional trim, safety pin decorative buttons to the front of the vest. Punch holes on both sides of the vest and close by lacing the sides with black ribbon. (Illustration 1-B)

Next, your child will need a long pair of white tube socks. Lay the socks on a flat surface and horizontally stripe them with 1-inch masking tape on both sides. Be sure and firmly press the masking tape to the socks. Paint the socks with a can of green spray paint. When the paint has thoroughly dried, remove the tape and you'll have a pair of green and white striped socks.

For pants, use a pair of green sweat pants. If you don't have green, dye a pair of white sweat pants green.

To assemble this outfit, have your child slip on his green and white striped socks. Next, put on the green sweat pants. The pants' legs are then pulled up to your child's knees to create the illusion of knee pants. Black shoes are next; and if so desired, silver buckles can be made out of cardboard and aluminum foil. Insert a piece of black felt between each buckle and secure the buckles to the shoes with either thread, elastic or string. (Illustration 2)

(2)

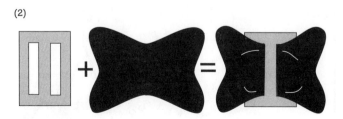

(3)

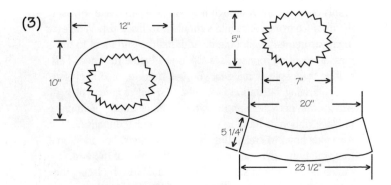

A white long-sleeved shirt is next. To this you will add a bow tie that is made from a long strip of black material. Turn up the collar of the shirt and tie the material around your child's neck as if you were tying a shoestring into a bow. The green vest is naturally placed over the shirt and held in place with a wide black belt.

A hat, while being optional, does add to the costume. During the month of March, most novelty stores and costume shops sell cardboard party hats that resemble leprechaun hats. Rather than make the hat, we suggest you just buy one as they are inexpensive. If you can't find one, make your own hat by cutting pieces out of poster board. (Illustration 3) Assemble the pieces with masking tape and cover with white glue and green felt. The hat band is made out of black felt with a large cardboard buckle covered with aluminum foil. A feather is always a nice finishing touch.

Dressing up as an Easter egg can be a festive way to celebrate this holiday.

MATERIALS NEEDED
* Contact cement
* Paint brush
* 1-inch foam rubber
* Butcher knife
* Yellow leotard & tights
* Yellow marabou
* Yellow feather boa (or yellow crepe paper)
* Purple spray paint

(1-A)

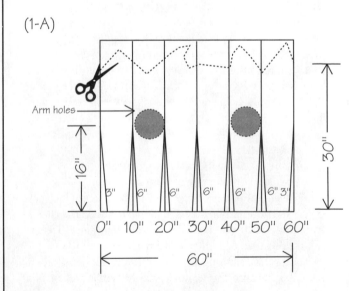

Foam rubber is a wonderful product that can be used to construct a multitude of unusual costumes. Once you master the basic techniques, you can make oversized fruits, vegetables, or other larger-than-life products.

The egg requires a rectangular piece of 1-inch foam rubber measuring 30 inches by 60 inches which is glued together along the 30-inch sides to form a cylinder and darted in at the bottom and cut jagged at the top.

To do this one must begin by marking every 10 inches along the bottom of the 60-inch side. Using the mark as the center of the base, draw a triangular wedge, the base of which should measure 6 inches and the height 16 inches. Note that the sides of the wedge curve inwards. (Illustration 1A) At the ends, however, draw a wedge the base of which should measure only 3 inches. Using a butcher knife cut out the wedges and at the top cut a jagged edge resembling a cracked eggshell.

With a 1-inch paint brush, brush contact cement along each side and bottom edge of the foam. Allow this to dry just enough that it is no longer wet to the touch. Don't try to glue the edges while they are still wet. When the glue is dry to the touch, glue the 30-inch sides together to form a cylinder and then dart in the bottom. (Illustration 1B)

Cut out the sections so that the arms will fit snugly in the holes because the eggshell will be supported in this manner. (Illustration 1A) Using purple spray paint, paint designs on the eggshell. Cover the glue seams with the painted decorations.

If you cannot buy a yellow leotard and tights use white ones and dye them. Pin a piece of yellow marabou around each wrist and ankle. If a yellow boa is available pin it around the neck and shoulders of the leotard. If a boa is not available, use strips of yellow crepe paper.

To make the hat, use a rectangular piece of 1-inch foam rubber measuring 12 inches by 24 inches. Repeat the same procedures used for making the egg except use illustration 2A as a guide. Note that the base of the wedge should measure 4 inches and the height 6 inches. When completed, the hat should resemble illustration 2B. This can be secured to the head by running a piece of string through the foam and tied under the chin.

(2-B)

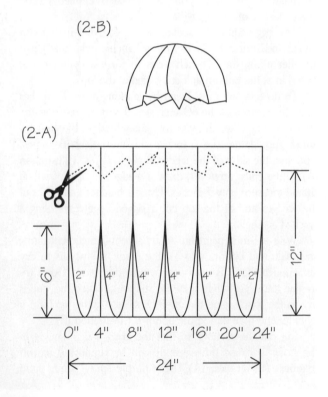

(2-A)

The Statue of Liberty is the symbol of freedom in America, and it makes for a wonderful costume for Fourth of July celebrations.

MATERIALS NEEDED
* Green material
* White glue
* Old telephone book
* Green spray paint
* Poster board
* Cord for belt
* Red and yellow crepe paper
* Foam rubber
* Contact cement
* Sandals
* Glitter sparkles

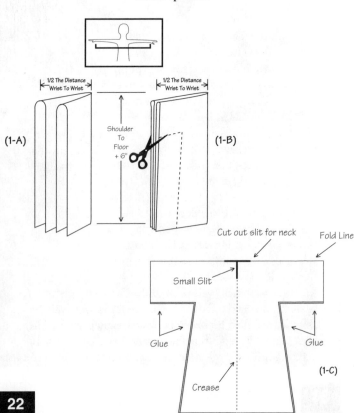

If possible, try to make this outfit out of green fabric which will resemble, as closely as possible, the color of weathered copper.

Measure the distance from your child's shoulder to her feet. Whatever the measurement is, double it and add 12 inches to this to get the length of material you will need to make the robe. Next, have your child stand with her arms out from her sides like a scarecrow. Measure from wrist to wrist to get the width of material you will need to make the robe.

Fold the material in half, first lengthwise and then again widthwise. (Illustration 1-A) Cut a piece out of the lower free corners as shown in illustration 1-B. Unfold the material widthwise revealing a bell-shaped pattern. (Illustration 1-C) Make an opening for the head by cutting a small slit in the center lengthwise fold. Also make a slit down the center front crease. It is always best not to make the openings too big. Start small and increase it gradually until your child can fit her head in easily. Glue the side seams shut by applying white glue about 1/2 inch away from the edge of the fabric and then press the two pieces of material together with your fingers. When the glue has dried, turn the robe inside out to hide the seams. The robe is belted in at the waist with a cord. Blouse any excess length over the cord.

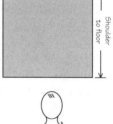

(2)

For the drape that hangs over the robe, take a piece of the same fabric used to make the robe and cut a large square, the sides of which should be the length of your child's shoulder to floor measurement. Taking two top corners, wrap the material around the body and tie the corners together over the left shoulder. (Illustration 2)

Three important parts of the Statue of Liberty costume are the tablet, the torch, and the headpiece. Let's start with the tablet. Take an old telephone book and spray paint it with green paint. The torch is nothing more than a piece of poster board or cardboard rolled into a conical shape and held in place with either white glue or tape. A piece of white rope should be glued around the open edge. Color the torch with the same paint that was used on the tablet. Red and yellow crepe paper or cellophane can be crushed about inside the cone to simulate the flame.

The spiked crown or headpiece is made from foam rubber. You will need a piece of foam rubber that is approximately 1 inch thick x 12 inches long x 5 inches wide. Using a magic marker and a ruler, mark off the triangular spikes on the foam by following illustration 3-A. With the base of each of the six spikes measuring 2 inches, the points will meet the other side of the foam at 1 inch, 3 inch, 5 inch, 7 inch, 9 inch, and 11 inches respectively. Once marked, use a sharp butcher's knife to cut away the excess foam (Illustration 3-B). Use a pair of scissors to cut off the square edges on the spikes to give them a more conical shape. Next, cut a piece of cardboard into a rectangle 1 inch x 14 inches. Now coat the cardboard and the spikes with contact cement and allow to dry thoroughly. Using contact cement, glue the cardboard to the base of the spikes, leaving 1 inch on either side free. Punch holes in the ends of the cardboard. Through these holes, thread elastic or string so that the crown can be tied around the head. (Illustration 3-C) Paint green and the crown is complete.

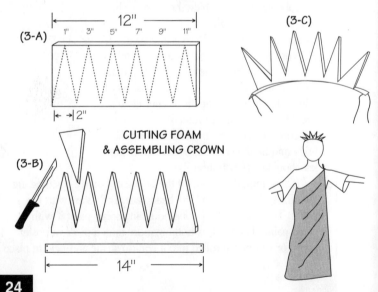

(3-A)   12"   (3-C)
1" 3" 5" 7" 9" 11"

2"

CUTTING FOAM
& ASSEMBLING CROWN

(3-B)

14"

Our patriotic hero, Yankee Doodle Dandy, is bound to add merriment to any Fourth of July festivity.

MATERIALS NEEDED
* White shirt and pants
* Masking tape
* Red spray paint
* Blue felt for vest
* Silver vinyl or white felt (for stars)
* White glue
* Red crepe paper (for bow tie & arm garters)
* Two small American flags

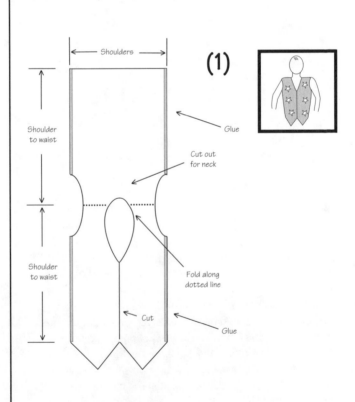

Shoulders

(1)

Shoulder to waist

Glue

Cut out for neck

Shoulder to waist

Fold along dotted line

Cut

Glue

(2)

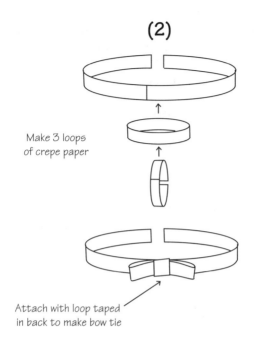

Make 3 loops
of crepe paper

Attach with loop taped
in back to make bow tie

Red-and-white striped pants are essential for this costume. Fabric shops sell this type of material, but it is almost impossible to make pants without sewing. Our costuming technique eliminates this problem. Lay your child's white pants on a flat surface and vertically stripe them in measured intervals with masking tape. Be sure to firmly press the masking tape to the pants. Dust the pants down with red spray paint. When the paint has dried, remove all the tape and, behold, you'll have a pair of red-and-white striped pants.

A blue vest can easily be turned into a patriotic waistcoat. Cut some stars out of white felt or silver vinyl and glue them to the vest. If you don't have an appropriate vest, one can easily be made out of blue felt. The width of the vest should be roughly the distance between the two shoulders, while the overall length should be twice the distance as measured from your child' shoulder to his waist. Following illustration

1, cut the vest and secure the appropriate edges with white glue. When the glue has dried, turn the vest inside out to hide the seams. Stars can be made out of white felt or silver vinyl and secured to the vest with glue.

Use red crepe paper to make a bow tie. (Illustration 2) Crepe paper can also be gathered on tape to form arm garters. (Illustration 3)

Paper Uncle Sam hats are available at novelty and costume stores. They are inexpensive, and we suggest that you just buy a hat. If you are unable to find one, one can be made out of poster board by following illustration 4. Cover the hat with white felt and vertically stripe it with masking tape. Spray paint the hat red and remove the tape. A hat band can be made out of blue crepe paper.

To finish this outfit, add a white shirt and two hand-held American flags, and your son or daughter is ready to march in any Fourth of July parade.

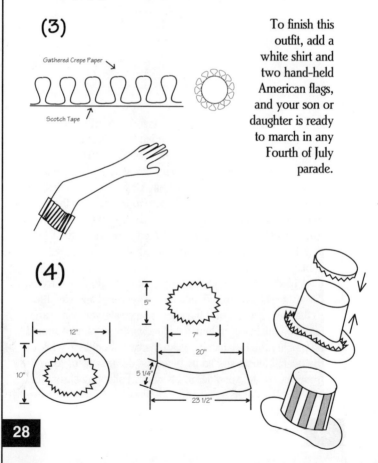

(3)

Gathered Crepe Paper

Scotch Tape

(4)

12"

10"

5"

7"

20"

5 1/4"

23 1/2"

This costume is suggested for Octoberfest celebrations. It could also be used for Hansel of *Hansel and Grethel.*

MATERIALS NEEDED
* Green, brown, tan, or gray pants
* Red or green ribbon (or yarn)
* White glue
* Red or green suspenders
* Felt (a contrasting color to the pants)
* White shirt
* Red or green knee-high socks
* Red ribbon for tie
* Lace-up shoes
* Hat

(1a)

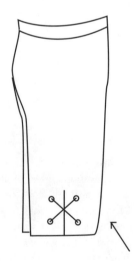

Cut off pants
at the knee

Red Stiching

(1b)

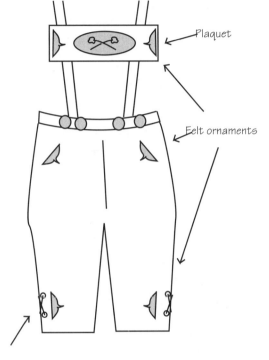

Plaquet

Felt ornaments

Red Stiching

Tyroleans wear lederhosen which are traditionally leather or heavy wool shorts. Most of the summer shorts that young boys wear will not work for this costume as they are made of cotton. Long pants that are made from either wool or corduroy have the right texture for imitating lederhosen. We suggest that you use this type of pants in either brown, tan, gray or green colors.

Cut the long pants off at the knee and glue a hem in them. Split the outside side seams of the pants about 2 inches. Hem the seams by using white glue. Next, punch holes on both sides of each seam and stitch up the holes with red or green ribbon or yarn. The stitch should resemble the letter X. (Illustration 1-A)

Secure a pair of red or green suspenders for the pants. Using some of the leftover fabric from the pants, make a plaquet for the suspenders. This can be safety pinned from behind to the suspenders. Using felt, cut out alpine designs and ornament the plaquet, the pockets, and bottom of the pants. Also safety pin 4 large metal buttons at the waist line to represent suspender buttons. (Illustration 1-B)

A white shirt, red or green knee high socks, and lace up shoes are also required. A piece of red ribbon is needed to create a ribbon tie. A Henry Higgins-type hat will complete the costume. The hat can be adorned with a decoration made with straw from a broom, some felt, a button, and some white glue. (Illustration 2) The straw and felt can be colored with magic markers and the decoration pinned to the hat. A piece of ribbon or felt can be added around the crown of the hat for added decoration.

(2)

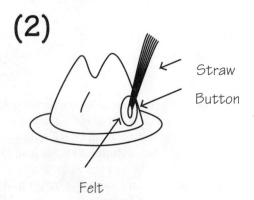

Straw

Button

Felt

The Grim Reaper is the medieval personification of death. At Halloween, he is a favorite character of children and adults alike.

MATERIALS NEEDED
* Black felt
* White glue
* Black & white make-up (or a skull mask)
* Green spray paint
* White cord or rope

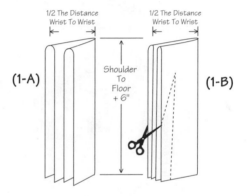

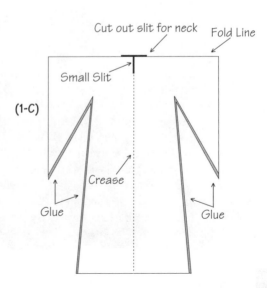

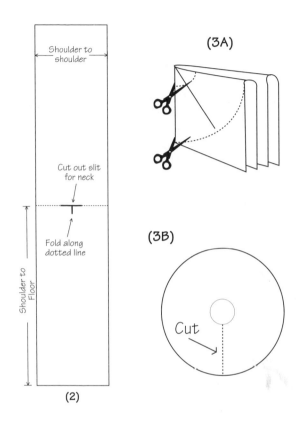

Shoulder to shoulder

(3A)

Cut out slit for neck

(3B)

Fold along dotted line

Shoulder to Floor

Cut

(2)

For the Grim Reaper, the more layers the better the costume will look. Besides the robe and cowl, we will also add a capelet and tabard to our costume.

Measure the distance from your child's shoulder to his feet. Whatever the measurement is, double it and add 12 inches to this to get the length of material you will need to make the robe. Have your child stand with his arms out from his sides like a scarecrow. Measure from wrist to wrist to get the width of material you will need to make the robe.

Fold the material in half, first lengthwise and then again widthwise. (Illustration 1-A) Cut a piece out of the lower free corners as shown in illustration 1-B. Unfold the material widthwise revealing a bell-shaped pattern. (Illustration 1-C) Make an opening for the head by cutting a small slit in the center of the lengthwise fold. Also make a slit down the center front crease. It is always best not to make the openings too big. Start small and increase it gradually until your child can fit his head in easily.

Next, glue the side seams shut by applying white glue about 1/2 inch away from the edge of the fabric and then press the two pieces of material together with your fingers. When the glue has dried, turn the robe inside out to hide the seams. Dust it down with green spray paint in order to give it an eerie look. Slip the robe on and draw it in around the waist with a colored cord. Draw up any excess length and blouse it over the cord. The sleeves may be too long, but don't cut them off. Instead, pleat them along the arm to give plenty of fullness. This can be done first with pins to get the desired length, then glue these pleats in place and remove the pins.

Using illustration 2 as a guide, make a tabard out of the same material that you used to make your outer robe. The width of the tabard should be roughly the distance between the two shoulders, while the overall length should be twice the distance as measured from shoulder to the floor. Cut a small T-shaped opening in the center of the material for your child's head. Dust the tabard down with the same

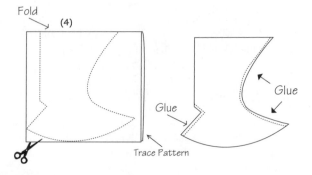

green spray paint that you used on the outer robe. The tabard is worn over the robe.

To make the capelet, use a full circle. This is simply done by folding the material into quarters. By using a piece of string as a guide, mark off a quarter circle. (Illustration 3-A) The size of your child will determine the radius of the circle. You will also need to cut out a small circle in the center for the neck. The radius of this will probably be about 2 inches. Cut the neck hole small at first and then trim until you have a good fit. You will also have to cut an opening in the circle. (Illustration 3-B) The capelet should also be painted the same as the robe. Safety pin in place around the neck.

Illustration 4 clearly shows you how to make a cowl. Just glue the appropriate edges together, let it dry, and by turning it inside out, it is ready to be worn. You will want to dust the hood down with some green paint.

You can use a skull mask, but for children we recommend make-up for better vision and comfort. This particular make-up is really not difficult if you follow our directions as shown on the following pages.

Outline the areas as shown in photo 1 with a black eyebrow pencil. Apply a coat of clown white over the entire face, excluding the penciled-in areas. (Photo 2) Fill in the outlined areas with black make-up as shown in photo 3. Draw in the skull and lip lines using a black eyebrow pencil. Blend in some yellow and brown make-up into portions of the clown white to create a bone-like color. (Photo 4) Powder the entire face with either a translucent powder or white baby powder and remove the excess with a soft brush.

A scythe is a necessary part of the Grim Reaper's costume. If you are not able to find a plastic one at a novelty or costume shop, one can be made with a mop stick, some cardboard, masking tape, and aluminum foil. With a scythe in his hand, your child is ready to haunt any house.

PHOTO #1

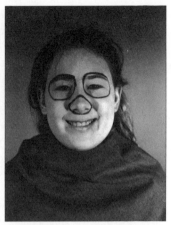

PHOTO #2

PHOTO #3

PHOTO #4

If you need a quick costume for your child, you can thank H.G. Wells for this one. It's one of those costumes that needs to be seen to be appreciated. It is not recommended for very young children.

MATERIALS NEEDED
* Dark suit
* White shirt
* Four-in-hand tie
* Sunglasses
* Gloves
* Surgical gauze
* Hat

Basically, any type of clothes can be worn with this outfit. We, however, recommend a dark suit. After your son is dressed, proceed to wrap surgical gauze around his head while allowing small yet adequate spaces for seeing, breathing, and hearing. The loose ends of the bandage can be held in place either by tucking in the edges or by carefully using safety pins.

A fedora is preferred over other types of hats, but a cap can work just as well. Practically any type of sunglasses will work for this costume, but if you can obtain the ones that also shield your eyes on the sides, these are the best.

During the times of Henry the VIII, this gruesome character was a familiar sight in London. We thought we would include him in our Halloween costume section to help round out our host of frightening friends.

MATERIALS NEEDED
* Black felt
* Black tights (or pants)
* Buttons for trim
* Lacings, e.g., rawhide, or black or brown shoelaces
* Black belt
* White glue
* Black woolly socks
* Black vinyl
* Toy ax

(1-A)   (1-B)

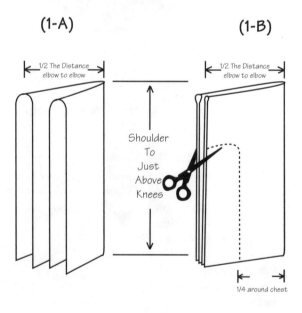

1/2 The Distance elbow to elbow

1/2 The Distance elbow to elbow

Shoulder
To
Just
Above
Knees

1/4 around chest

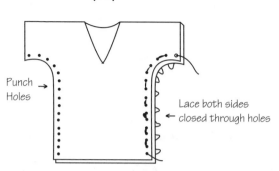

Punch → Holes

Lace both sides ← closed through holes

Measure the distance from your child's shoulder to just above his knees. Whatever the measurement is, double it to get the length of material you will need to make the tunic. Have your child stand with his arms out from his sides like a scarecrow. Measure from elbow to elbow to get the width of material you will need to make the tunic.

Fold the material in half, first lengthwise and then again widthwise. (Illustration 1-A) Using illustration 1-B as a guide, cut out the main part of the tunic. Now, unfold the material widthwise to reveal a T-shaped pattern. Next, you must cut an opening for the head. In the center front cut out a "V" large enough just to get the head through. (Illustration 1-C) The tunic will fit better if you also slightly round the back of the opening where the neck is. Punch holes along the sides and lace shut with rawhide, or black or brown shoelaces. Silver or brass buttons can be pinned to the tunic for added effect. (See picture.)

Following illustration 2, cut out two pieces of black vinyl that will fit comfortably around your son's wrists. Holes should be punched into each side of the vinyl and then these cuffs should be laced around your child's wrists by using either rawhide, or black or brown shoelaces.

An executioner would not be in character unless he wore the traditional black hood. For the hood, follow

(2)

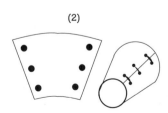

illustration 3. Cut out two identical pieces of black felt. Apply white glue about 1/2 inch around the top edge and then press the two pieces of material together with your fingers. When the glue has dried, turn the hood inside out to hide the seams. Next, cut out two large eye holes so that your child's vision is not impaired.

Executioners are known for carrying an ax. During the season of Halloween, toy axes are sold in novelty, costume, and toy stores. We recommend that you just purchase one. If, however, you can't locate a toy ax, one can easily be made by securing a piece of cardboard to a wooden dowel, and then cover the cardboard with aluminum foil.

To assemble the outfit, have your child first slip on his black tights or pants. He can wear his regular shoes with this costume and cover them with a pair of men's black woolly socks. The black tunic comes next, followed by the wrist cuffs and hood. Belt in the tunic with a man's wide black belt. Add extra belt holes if necessary, but don't cut off the excess length. Just wrap this about as is shown in the photograph. With the fake ax in hand, your youngster is ready to scare friends and neighbors.

(3)

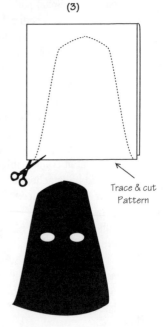

Trace & cut Pattern

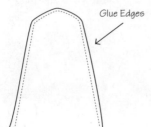

Glue Edges

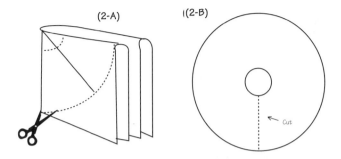

(2-A)　　　　((2-B)

← Cut

Measure the distance from your child's shoulder to her feet. Whatever the measurement is, double it and add 12 inches to get the length of material you will need to make the dress. Have your child stand with her arms out from her sides like a scarecrow. Measure from wrist to wrist to get the width of material you will need to make the dress.

Fold the material in half, first lengthwise and then again widthwise. (Illustration 1-A) Cut a piece out of the lower free corners as is shown in illustration 1-B. Unfold the material widthwise revealing a bell-shaped pattern. (Illustration 1-C.) You will now need to make an opening for the head. Cut a small slit in the center of the lengthwise fold. Next, cut a small slit down the center front crease. It is always best not to make these openings too big. Start small and increase it gradually until your child can fit her head in easily.

Using white glue, glue the sides and underarm seams by applying it about 1/2 inch away from the edge of the fabric and then press the two pieces of material together with your fingers. When the glue has dried, turn the fabric inside out to hide the seams. You can wear a black leotard underneath this to cover the arms. This is good for those cold Halloween nights.

To make the capelet, use a full circle. This is simply done by folding the material into quarters. By using a piece of string as a guide, mark off a quarter circle. The size of

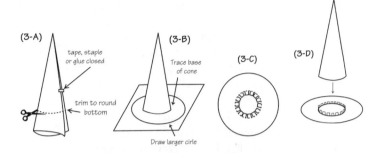

(3-A) tape, staple or glue closed
trim to round bottom

(3-B) Trace base of cone
Draw larger cirle

(3-C)

(3-D)

your child will determine the radius of the circle. You will also need to cut out a small circle in the center for the neck. The radius of this will probably be about 2 inches. (Illustration 2-A) Cut the neck hole small at first and then trim until you have a good fit. You will also have to cut an opening in the circle. (Illustration 2-B) Pin in place around the neck.

Around Halloween, novelty and department stores as well as costume shops sell nice looking witch's hats. They are so inexpensive, we suggest you buy one. If not, you can make one by using two pieces of poster board. Form one of the pieces of cardboard into a cone which will fit over your child's head. Staple, glue or tape the overlapping pieces together to hold it in place. Trim the bottom edge even. (Illustration 3-A)

Place the open end of the cone on the second piece of poster board and draw a circle around the edge of the cone. When you are finished, remove the cone and sketch a larger circle about the first circle. (Illustration 3-B) The distance between the two circles is the width of the brim. Now draw another circle about 1 inch within the smaller circle. Cut out the smallest and largest of the circles. Cut slits from the inside circle 1 inch to the circle that was the size of the open end of the cone. (Illustration 3-C) These slits will allow you to bend the cardboard and form a flange that can be taped or hot glued to the base of the cone. (Illustration 3-D) Cover the hat with black felt. Use black crepe paper to make a hat band.

A good make-up job will help make your little witch look more sinister. A long rubber witch nose and pointed chin can be bought at a costume shop or novelty store. Apply a thin coat of spirit gum to the inside edge of the nose and chin where they will make contact with the face. Allow the spirit gum to become tacky before placing the false nose and chin in place. (Photo 1)

Use a sponge to apply an even coat of green make-up over your child's entire face. Be careful not to damage the sculptured nose and chin. Use a darker tone make-up in colors such as black, brown or gray to shadow in areas as is shown in photo 2. Apply a translucent powder over the entire face. Allow it to set for a few minutes before brushing off the excess powder.

Add a black wig or tease your child's hair and then spray it with black hair spray.

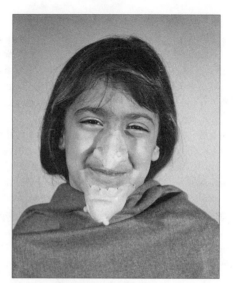

PHOTO #1

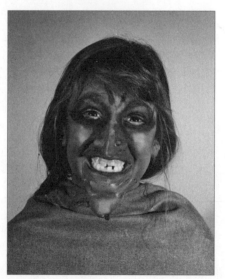

PHOTO #2

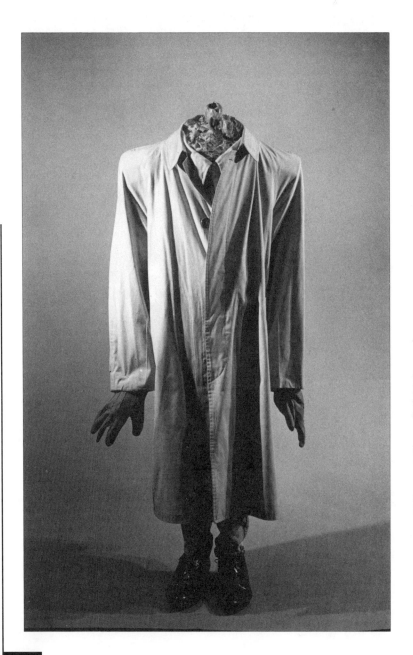

While this costume is an attention-getter by itself, it is also the perfect companion to the executioner.

* A man's white shirt
* A man's old raincoat
* Plastic ice cream bucket (one gallon)
* Hot glue gun
* Cardboard
* Duct tape
* Paper towels
* Cardboard paper towel tube
* Red paint
* Gloves

Obtain a round plastic ice cream bucket, the top of which is able to fit over your child's head as if it were a helmet. Have your child put the bucket over his head, and notice where his eyes would appear underneath the plastic bucket. Use a marking pen and sketch outlines for eye holes

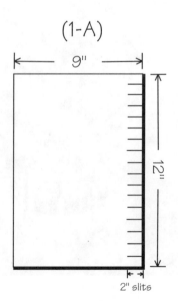

(1-A)

9"

12"

2" slits

onto the plastic. It is better to make the eye openings smaller and enlarge them if necessary rather than vice versa. Use scissors or a matte knife to cut out the openings.

Cut two pieces of stiff cardboard 12 inches by 9 inches. Cut 2-inch-long slits along a 12-inch end of each piece. (Illustration 1-A) Bend the slit pieces at right angles to form a flange which can be duct taped to the bucket. Bend the cardboard to resemble a shoulder and tape the flanged edge to the bucket. (Illustration 1-B) When the cardboard pieces

(1-B)

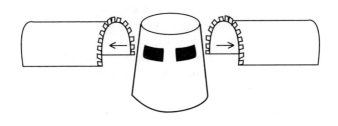

Duct tape cardboard
tube to bucket

Duct tape flange
to bucket

(1-C)

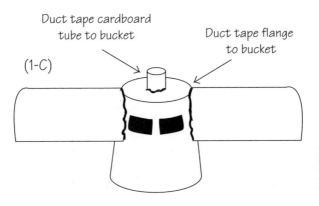

are fastened to the bucket as shown, and the bucket is placed on the head, the tubes will simulate a person's shoulders, while the bucket will simulate the neck. (Illustration 1-C) Using duct tape, attach a small section of a cardboard paper towel tube to the top center of the bucket. This tube will represent the back bone. Glue paper towels on top of the bucket and color it with red paint, and drip hot glue on top. Paint the tube representing the back bone a natural color. A bit of artificial blood splattered on the shirt and coat near the neck will add to the gory effect.

With the bucket and cardboard shoulders in place over your child's head, a man's large white shirt should be split up the back and glued to the cardboard shoulder pieces. Separate the front of the shirt so that the child will have clear vision through the eye holes in the bucket. Glue the front of the shirt so that the opening does not impair the child's vision. Remove the sleeves if necessary. To finish the costume, have your son or daughter wear a man's old raincoat, to which a pair of stuffed gloves are pinned to the ends of the sleeves. If your child can walk safely with them, a pair of men's shoes are worn over your child's shoes.

DRACULA

Lock your doors and turn on the lights, for here comes Bram Stoker's immortal creation—Dracula. This legendary creature of the night is probably the world's most renowned vampire and, thanks to Hollywood, boys of all ages desire to masquerade as the notorious count.

MATERIALS NEEDED
* Wide black & red material (for cape & lining)
* White shirt with long sleeves
* Black pants
* White bow tie (or white grosgrain ribbon)
* Red ribbon
* Junk jewelry
* White glue
* Make-up:
  Black hair spray
  Black eyebrow pencil
  Black & white make-up
  Red lipstick
  Fangs

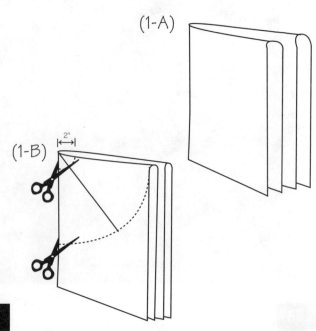

(1-A)

(1-B)

2"

56

Here are two options for creating this costume; you can either purchase a child's full dress suit, which would certainly add to the professionalism of his costume, or put the basic outfit together yourself. The reason you may want to consider purchasing a child's full dress suit lies in our experience and knowledge of the costume trade. Many people do not realize it, but the formal rental business drastically changes lines from year to year. Local tuxedo houses (check your city's yellow pages in the telephone book) often sell out-of-date clothes at a very reasonable price. So, if you don't have what you need or if you want the best for your youngster, you might want to consider our first option.

Nevertheless, to put the basic costume together yourself, your child will need a white shirt, dark shoes, a pair of dark pants (preferably black) and a white bow tie or a piece of white grosgrian ribbon. Other than this, there are three things necessary to complete a good Dracula character: a medallion, a cape and, most important, a good make-up job.

The medallion can be nothing more than a piece of junk jewelry that is attached to a piece of red ribbon, either with glue or tied in place with thread. The ribbon can be secured around the neck with a safety pin. When you are finished, turn up the collar of the white shirt and use white ribbon to make a bow tie.

(1-C)

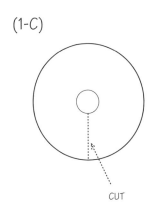

CUT

(2)

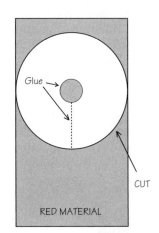

Glue

CUT

RED MATERIAL

Buying a cape is also a very practical option. Toy stores and costume shops generally sell suitable Dracula capes for less money then you can buy the material. Nevertheless, if you cannot find one, you can make one by cutting a full circle out of black material and lining it with red material. To do this, fold the black material into quarters. (Illustration 1-A) Using a piece of string as a guide, mark off a quarter of a circle with a radius about 2 inches. This will fit the neck. Mark off another quarter of a circle with the longest radius the width of the material will allow. (Illustration 1-B) Cut a slit for the center front opening along one radius. Unfold the material and you should have a black cape. (Illustration 1-C) To make a red lining, lay this flat on the red material, and using white glue, glue the neck hole and center front opening only, leaving the bottom open. (Illustration 2) When dry, cut out the red material around the black cape and turn inside out. Use a safety pin to secure the cape around the neck.

By far, the make-up is the most important feature of this costume. Follow the simple step-by-step instructions for a very effective make-up job. Wash your child's hair and comb it straight back, allowing it ample time to dry tight to his head. A touch of hair spray will hold it into position. If your youngster doesn't have dark or black hair, it can easily be tinted with black-colored hair spray and slicked back. Use a black eyebrow pencil to sketch a widow's peak on the forehead. (Photo 1) Using the black pencil, draw dark piercing eyebrows and then apply a thin base coat of white make-up (such as clown white) over the entire face, excluding the penciled-in areas. (Photo 2). Apply either black or gray make-up with a brush or a sponge to shade in the areas around the eyes, nose, and below the cheekbones as shown in photo 3. A dash of red lipstick over the lips and an inexpensive pair of white fangs set the mood for this gothic character. (Photo 4)

PHOTO #1

PHOTO #2

PHOTO #3

PHOTO #4

Thanks to a slew of fright films made in Hollywood in recent years, the werewolf has once again become a popular monster. No matter how old or how young you are, the werewolf made famous by Lon Chaney, Jr. still serves best to characterize this frightful monster.

MATERIALS NEEDED
* Flannel shirt
* Corduroy pants
* Hemp rope
* Make-up

This is probably one of the simplest costumes to put together, for it requires just a few pieces of modern clothing. Chances are, you already have a flannel shirt and corduroy pants in your son's wardrobe. Other than a piece of rope, which will be used as a belt, your son is all set for this costume. The tricky part, however, is the make-up.

Here is a list of make-up supplies you will need for the werewolf: fangs, black and brown make-up, a rubber werewolf nose, a yard of brown crepe hair, spirit gum, spirit gum remover, and brown colored hair spray. All of these materials are standard make-up items and are available from any reputable costume shop.

Apply a thin coat of spirit gum to the inside edge of a rubber werewolf nose where it will make contact with the face. Allow the spirit gum to become tacky before attaching the false nose. (Photo 1) Next, apply brown make-up to the areas of the face as shown in (Photo 2), page 63.

Crepe hair is used by professional actors to make wigs, beards and mustaches. In its original state, crepe hair comes in the form of a thick braided rope. To use it you must first

Photo #1

Photo #2

cut the string and unravel the braid; the hair will be curly. To remove the curls, separate the hairs with your fingers and straighten by pressing with a steam iron. Pull off sections about three inches long and apply to the face as described in the next step.

Use an eyebrow pencil to divide the forehead into three equal horizontal sections. At the first line just above the eyebrows apply a thin coat of spirit gum across the forehead, about an inch wide. Apply 3-inch-long pieces of crepe hair vertically to the spirit gum. Glue only the lower part of this layer of hair. Move the upper part of the layer away from the face and apply spirit gum along line 2. Once again, apply 3-inch-long pieces of crepe hair along line 2, and repeat this procedure with line 3. Gently brush all the crepe hair upwards so that it blends together, and the top layers blend into the real hair. (Photo 3) You can use a light coat of brown-colored hair spray to blend the crepe hair on the forehead with the child's natural hair.

Starting under the eyes, using the same procedures above, apply spirit gum and crepe hair over the entire face and neck. (Photo 4)

Blend black make-up into the brown areas around the eyes, ears and mouth to achieve a leathery effect. Use a sharp knife to change a plastic set of fangs into realistic werewolf teeth by scratching and cutting some of the portions away from the shiny white teeth. Rub a little black and brown make-up into the crevices.

Apply crepe hair and make-up to the hands, and color the fingernails black for a more realistic werewolf. Rubber werewolf ears are optional.

When you have completed the make-up, tell your son not to forget to howl whenever there is a full moon.

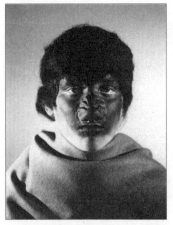

Photo #3

Photo #4

Scarecrows are often associated with the fall harvest and thus make a good Halloween costume. Some children, however, are only familiar with one friendly scarecrow from *The Wizard of Oz*.

MATERIALS NEEDED
* A man's colorful flannel shirt
* Colorful patches
* Jeans
* Work gloves
* A man's pair of brown woolly socks
* White glue
* Yellow crepe paper
* Thick white rope
* Felt hat

As you can probably tell from our list of materials, most of these items are probably already in your family's wardrobe, or they can be purchased at a reasonable cost at a secondhand clothing store.

Attach various colored patches to a man's flannel shirt and your child's jeans by using glue. Using a black magic marker, draw stitch marks around the patches.

Instead of using straw in the scarecrow's outfit, try stripping yellow crepe paper. Glue it around the cuffs of the shirt and pants. You should also glue some crepe paper straw around the collar of the shirt. Make a slit in the top of an old felt hat, and glue some fake straw in this opening. Also add some crepe paper straw to a pair of work gloves.

To assemble this outfit, have your child put on the jeans and the oversized flannel shirt. The tail of the shirt should remain outside the pants. Tie a piece of thick rope around the child's waist, and blouse the shirt up and over the rope. A man's pair of brown woolly socks should be worn over the shoes and a piece of rope should be tied around the ankles to create booties.

You may wish to make a head covering for the scarecrow. This can be made out of very sheer material cut into a circle. Place the circle of fabric on top of the child's head and secure it at the neck with a piece of soft rope. The area surrounding the face can be cut away so it doesn't impair your child's vision. If the head covering doesn't appeal to you, just use make-up. Use an eyebrow pencil to create triangles around the eyes and stitch marks around the mouth. With the hat and gloves in place, your child is ready to add merriment to any occasion.

MUMMY

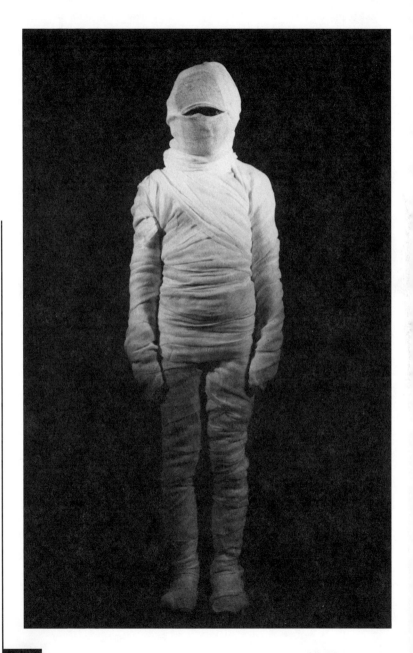

Ask any child to name some of Hollywood's greatest monsters and you can be sure that the mummy will be one of them. Torn from his Egyptian tomb, this unstoppable creature is bound to terrify any party.

MATERIALS NEEDED
* Long johns
* White glue
* Cheesecloth
* Pair of tennis shoes
* Old newspapers
* Plastic wrap

It is best to construct this costume with a top and bottom, otherwise your child will be encased in a one-piece body suit with no openings. Begin by stuffing both the top and bottom of the long johns with newspaper to approximate the size and shape of the child. The newspaper should be rolled and covered with plastic wrap. After the long johns are stuffed, cover them with a thin coat of white glue and wrap them with cheesecloth. We suggest cheesecloth because it is far less expensive than gauze bandages. After the glue has dried remove the newspaper and plastic stuffing.

To assemble, have your child put the pants on first, then his shoes, and then the tops to the long johns. With extra strips of cheesecloth, wrap the shoes, hands and face. Loose ends can be held in place by tucking in the edges or by carefully using safety pins. If you wish, however, you can prepare a pair of gloves for the hands and a ski hat for the head in a similar way as the long johns. Whichever way you choose, make certain that you allow enough space between the wrappings for your child to see, hear and breathe easily.

PILGRIM BOY

During the last few weeks of November, school children are often asked to dress up as pilgrims and partake in the famous Thanksgiving Day celebration. If your son is asked to be in this type of school production, here is an easy way to construct a pilgrim's costume.

MATERIALS NEEDED
* Dark suit
* Long white socks
* White and black felt
* Black shoes
* Cardboard hat or poster board
* Masking tape
* White glue

(1)

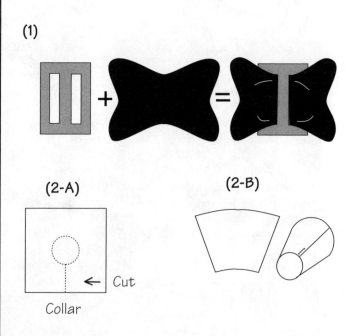

(2-A)

← Cut

Collar

(2-B)

(3)

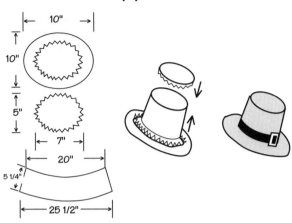

A dark-colored suit is the basic item you will need to make a pilgrim's outfit for your son. Let's begin with the pants.

In order to make a pair of knickers, turn up the pants' legs and hold them in place just below the knee with rubber bands. Add long white socks, which should come up to your child's knees, and then slip on a pair of black shoes. Make shoe buckles out of cardboard and cover them with aluminum foil. Insert a piece of black felt between each buckle and secure the buckles to the shoes with either thread, elastic or string. (Illustration 1)

To make a pilgrim's coat, use a dark colored suit jacket. Fold over the lapels and pin in place with safety pins. Cut out a square of white felt. A circle must be cut out of the center of the cloth in order to fit around the child's neck. Once the circle is cut out, slit the material. (Illustration 2-A) You will also need to make cuffs out of two pieces of white felt. These should be safety pinned around the cuffs of the coat. (Illustration 2-B)

Make a large cardboard buckle and cover it with aluminum foil. Attach around the waist with a strip of black felt pinned in the back.

For a pilgrim's hat, we recommend that you just buy a

cheap cardboard hat and modify it. Costume shops usually sell cheap top hats or Uncle Sam hats which, when modified, can easily resemble a pilgrim's hat. The pilgrim's hat is all black and has a buckle in the front. If you buy a hat and it is any other color than black, cover it with white glue and then black felt. Then, just make a big cardboard buckle, cover it with aluminum foil, and attach it to the front of the hat with a strip of black felt glued together at the back. To make your own hat, cut pieces out of poster board following illustration 3. Assemble the pieces with masking tape and cover with white glue and black felt.

A cape may be cut from black felt and pinned in place. To do this, fold the felt into quarters by folding it in half, first lengthwise and then again widthwise. Using a piece of string as a guide, mark off a quarter of a circle from the closed corner with a radius of about 2 inches. This will fit the neck. Mark off another quarter of a circle with the longest radius the width of the material will allow. (Illustration 4) Cut a slit for the center front opening along one radius. Unfold the material and you should have a black cape. Safety pin the cape around the neck under the collar.

(4)

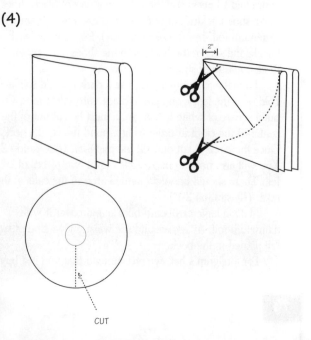

CUT

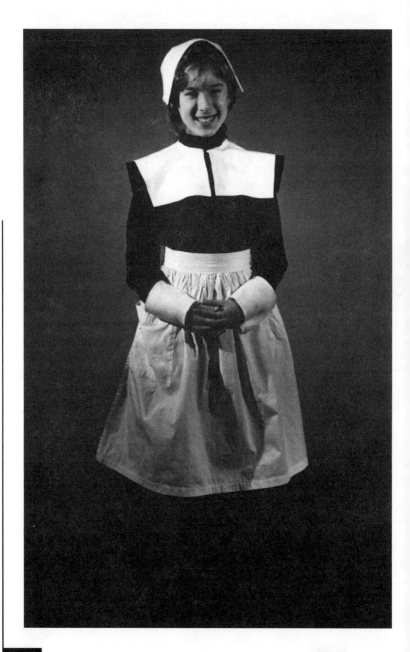

Besides being necessary for Thanksgiving pageants, Puritans may be required for plays. If you're ever required to costume your daughter for a production, the following will prove very helpful for those parents who cannot sew.

MATERIALS NEEDED
* Black long sleeved leotard or black turtleneck sweater
* Black felt (for dress)
* White felt (for collar, cuffs and bonnet)
* White apron

To know how much black felt you will need to make the dress, measure the distance from your daughter's shoulder to the floor. Whatever the measurement is, double it to get the length of material you will need to make the dress. To get the width, measure the distance from shoulder to shoulder and add 18 inches.

Fold the material in half, first lengthwise and then again widthwise as shown in illustration 1-A. Measure the distance from your daughter's nape of the neck to her waist. From the upper closed corner measure over 1/2 the shoulder-to-shoulder measurement. From that point, cut parallel to the edge the length of the measurement from the nape of the neck to her waist. Starting at that point cut towards the lower free corners as shown in illustration 1-B.

Unfold the material widthwise. Make an opening for the head by cutting a slit in the center of the lengthwise fold. Also, make a slit down the center front crease. It is always best not to make the openings too big. Start small and increase it gradually until your child can fit her head in easily. Glue the side seams from the waist to the floor by applying white glue about 1/2 inch away from the edge of the fabric and then press the two pieces of material together with your fingers. (Illustration 1-C) When the glue has dried, turn the robe inside out to hide the seams. This is worn over the black turtleneck to complete the basic dress. A white apron is worn over this.

(1-A)

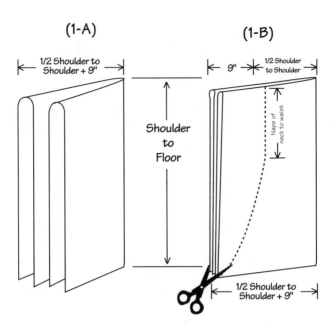

1/2 Shoulder to Shoulder + 9"

(1-B)

9"

1/2 Shoulder to Shoulder

Shoulder to Floor

Nape of neck to waist

1/2 Shoulder to Shoulder + 9"

(1-C)

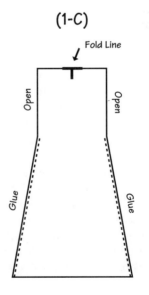

Fold Line

Open

Open

Glue

Glue

To make the collar, cut out a square of white felt. A circle must be cut out of the center of the cloth in order to fit around the child's neck. Once the circle is cut out, slit the material. (Illustration 2-A) You will also need to make cuffs out of two pieces of white felt. These should be safety pinned around the wrists. (Illustration 2-B)

The bonnet is a rectangle of white felt measuring appoximately 12 1/2 inches by 11 inches. It should be cut, safety pinned at the back and worn as shown. (Illustration 3)

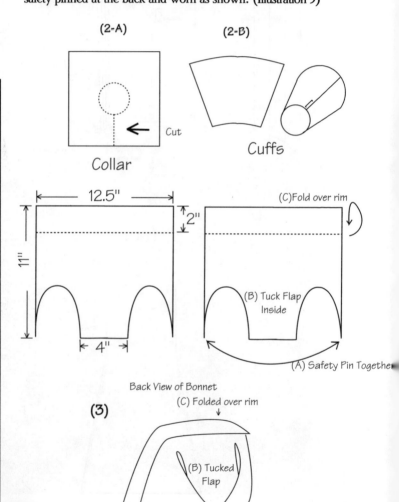

(2-A)

(2-B)

Cut

Collar

Cuffs

12.5"

2"

11"

4"

(C)Fold over rim

(B) Tuck Flap
Inside

(A) Safety Pin Together

Back View of Bonnet

(3)

(C) Folded over rim

(B) Tucked
Flap

Safety Pin

Besides being popular at Halloween, an Indian costume is often necessary for Thanksgiving plays and is useful for scouting events.

MATERIALS NEEDED
* Tan or brown felt
* Blue, black or red felt (for loin cloth)
* Rawhide or brown shoelaces
* Brown leather belt
* Colored marking pens or paints
* Feathers, fake fur

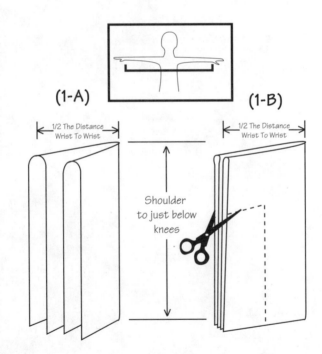

(1-A)   (1-B)

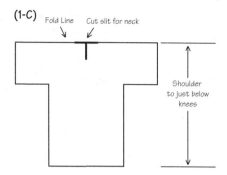

(1-C) Fold Line   Cut slit for neck

Shoulder
to just below
knees

This particular outfit calls for a quantity of felt in a color such as tan or brown. If this fabric is not available, any suede-like material will do. During the end of the 19th century, it was common for Indians to make shirts out of muslin which was then painted with visionary designs. We, however, recommend felt.

Measure the distance from your child's shoulder to just below his knees. Whatever the measurement is, double it to get the length of the material you will need to make the tunic. Have your child stand with his arms out from his sides like a scarecrow. Measure from wrist to wrist to get the width of material you will need to make the tunic.

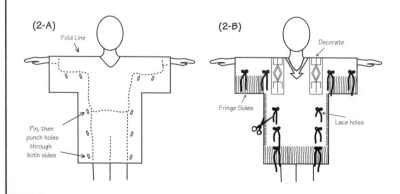

(2-A)
Fold Line

Pin, then
punch holes
through
both sides

(2-B)
Decorate

Fringe Sides

Lace holes

Fold the material in half, first lengthwise and then again widthwise. (Illustration 1-A) Cut a piece out of the lower free corners as shown in illustration 1-B. Make an opening for the head by cutting a slit in the center lengthwise fold. Also make a slit down the center front crease. (Illustration 1-C)

Slip the material over the head with the arms extended. The pieces of material that are hanging over the arms can temporarily be pinned to form a sleeve which is just wide enough to comfortably fit the arms. The remaining material hanging below the arms will later be cut to form fringe.

(3)

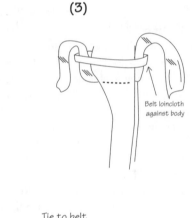

Belt loincloth
against body

(4)

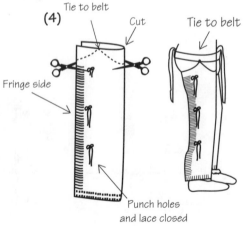

Tie to belt

Cut

Tie to belt

Fringe side

Punch holes
and lace closed

Place the pins evenly on both sleeves. Be sure to allow ample room for the movement of the arms. Also evenly pin the tunic in at the sides. (Illustration 2-A)

Now punch two corresponding holes next to each other on the front and back where each pin is. The sleeves and the sides may now be laced together with rawhide or brown shoelaces. Now fringe the edges of the sleeves up toward the arm and stop 1 inch before you hit the lacing. The ends of the sleeves may also be fringed. Also fringe the bottom and sides. (Illustration 2-B)

A brown leather belt should now be secured to your child's waist. A loincloth may be made from a rectangular piece of material. The width of the material should be one-half of the person's waist size and the length should be determined by measuring the following distances: In the front from below the knees up to the belt and towards the body, then between the legs and up the back over the belt and down to below the knees. (Illustration 3)

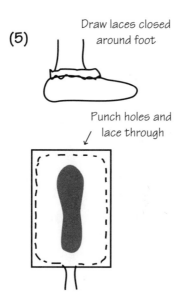

(5) Draw laces closed around foot

Punch holes and lace through

The leggings are made from two rectangular pieces of material, the length of which is the distance between the hip and the ankle. The width should be wide enough to comfortably wrap around the leg and have enough additional material to accommodate the lacing and fringe. The leggings can be assembled the same as the sleeves by punching holes and lacing. Once assembled, fringe the leggings the same as the sleeves. Place the leggings on the leg so that the top edge of the outside of the leggings can be tied to the belt around the child's waist. The excess material on the inside of the legging may be trimmed away to fit the child. (Illustration 4)

The headband is made by using a strip of material and tied around the forehead. Add a feather or two if desired.

For shoes, make moccasins by following illustration 5. Punch holes around the material and lace with rawhide or brown shoelaces. This can be made large enough to fit over your child's shoes.

All articles should be decorated with colored marking pens, paints, beads and fake fur.

INDIAN GIRL

Much like the Indian Boy costume, this outfit is perfect for young ladies who wish to participate in Thanksgiving plays.

* Tan or brown felt
* Rawhide or brown shoelaces
* Colored marking pens or paints
* Feathers, fake fur

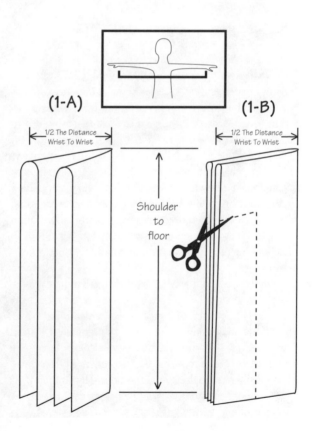

(1-A)

(1-B)

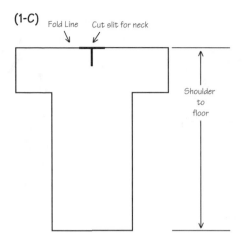

(1-C)   Fold Line   Cut slit for neck

Shoulder
to
floor

Measure the distance from your child's shoulder to the floor. Whatever the measurement is, double it to get the length of material you will need to make the dress. Next, have your child stand with her arms out from her sides like a scarecrow. Measure from wrist to wrist to get the width of material you will need to make the dress.

Fold the material in half, first lengthwise and then again widthwise. (Illustration 1-A) Cut a piece out of the lower free corners as shown in illustration 1-B. Make an opening for the head by cutting a slit in the center lengthwise fold. Also make a slit down the center front crease. (Illustration 1-C) It is always best not to make the openings too big. Start small and increase it gradually until your child can fit her head in easily.

Slip the material over the head with the arms extended. The pieces of material that are hanging over the arms can temporarily be pinned to form a sleeve which is just wide enough to comfortably fit the arms. The remaining material hanging below the arms will later be cut to form fringe. Be sure to allow ample room for the movement of the arms. Also, evenly pin the dress in at the sides. (Illustration 2-A)

Now punch two corresponding holes next to each other on the front and back where each pin is. The sleeves and

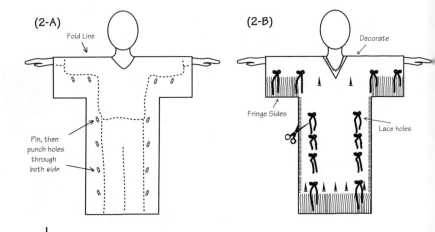

(2-A)
Fold Line

Pin, then punch holes through both side

(2-B)
Decorate

Fringe Sides

Lace holes

the sides may now be laced together with rawhide or brown shoelaces. Now fringe the edges of the sleeves up toward the arm and stop 1 inch before you hit the lacing. The ends of the sleeves may also be fringed. Also fringe the bottom and sides. (Illustration 2-B)

The headband is made by using a strip of material and tied around the forehead. Add a feather or two if desired.

For shoes, make moccasins. (Illustration 3) Punch holes around the material and lace with rawhide or brown shoelaces. This can be made large enough to fit over your child's shoes.

All articles should be decorated with colored marking pens, paints, beads and fake fur.

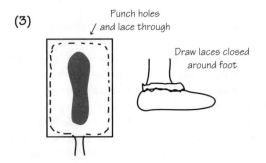

(3)
Punch holes and lace through

Draw laces closed around foot

ANGEL

ngel costumes are particularly popular during the month of December. If your child's school or church group is presenting a Christmas pageant, our easy to follow, step-by-step instructions will appear to be heavenly sent.

MATERIALS NEEDED
* Plenty of soft white material
* White glue
* White sheer material
* Sequins or gold Christmas garland
* Aluminum wire
* Fancy gold cord

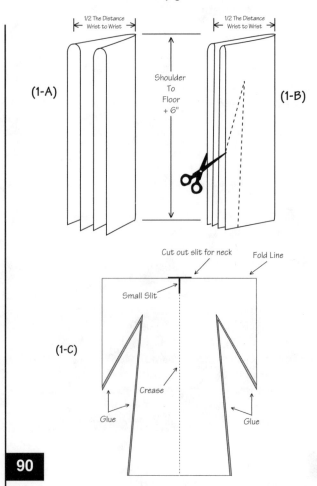

Measure the distance from your child's shoulder to her feet. Whatever the measurement is, double it and add 12 inches to get the length of material you will need to make the robe. Have your child stand with her arms out from her sides like a scarecrow. Measure from wrist to wrist to get the width of material you will need to make the robe.

Fold the material in half, first lengthwise and then again widthwise. (Illustration 1-A) Cut a piece out of the lower free corners following illustration 1-B. Unfold the material widthwise revealing a bell-shaped pattern. (Illustration 1-C) You will now need to make an opening for the head. Cut a small slit in the center of the lengthwise fold. Next, cut a small slit down the center front crease. Remember, it is best not to make these openings too big. Start small and increase it gradually until your child can fit her head in easily. Using white glue, glue the edges by applying it about 1/2 inch away from the edge of the fabric and then press the two pieces of material together with your fingers. When this has dried, turn the fabric inside out to hide the seams.

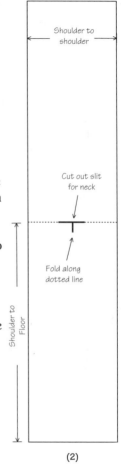

(2)

Next, make a tabard. A tabard is simply a rectangular piece of material. The width is the same as the distance between the two shoulders and the length is twice the distance as measured from shoulder to floor. A "T" shape is cut in the center for the head. (Illustration 2)

For the wings, we suggest you buy them at your local

novelty store or costume shop. If you can't acquire a pair, they can be made easily from cardboard covered with white felt, and decorated with glue and glitter. (Illustration 3) Four holes should be punched in the center panel between the wings. Through these holes thread elastic to form two loops. Secure the wings to your child's back by placing an arm through each loop, similar to the way a knapsack is worn.

To make a halo, use aluminum wire. Form a small circle —head size—within a large one as shown in illustration 4. Connect the circles with duct tape. Sequins or garland should be wrapped and glued around the large circle of wire forming the halo.

Slip the robe on first and then the wings. A cord should be worn around the waist and any excess length of the robe bloused over it. Put the tabard on next. This will conceal the center panel connecting the wings. Don't forget the halo!

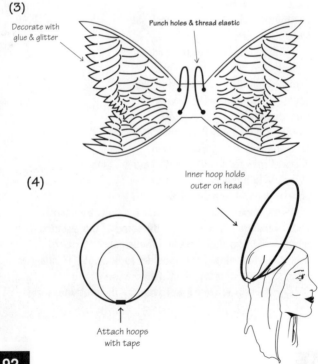

(3)

Decorate with glue & glitter

Punch holes & thread elastic

(4)

Inner hoop holds outer on head

Attach hoops with tape

Variations of this outfit can be used to costume most of the boys in Christmas pageants, including such figures as Joseph and the shepherds.

MATERIALS NEEDED
* Drapery casements (earth tone colors such as brown and gray)
* Strips of assorted fabrics
* Sandals

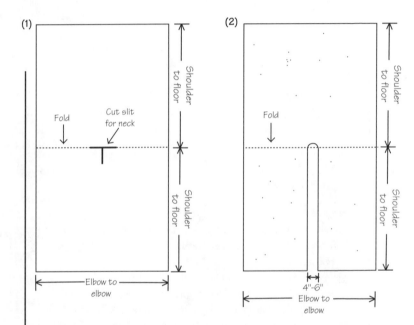

Let's begin with the under-robe. The under-robe is essentially a poncho. Measure the distance from your child's shoulder to his feet. Whatever the measurement is, double it to get the length of material you will need to make the under-robe. Next, have your child stand with his arms out from his sides like a scarecrow. Measure from elbow to elbow to get the width of material you will need to make the under-robe. Rather than using felt, which we have used

(3-A)

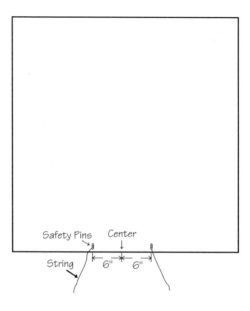

in most of the other costumes, we suggest that you use drapery casements in earth tone colors. Fold the material in half lengthwise and put a slit in the center just large enough to fit the head. (Illustration 1)

Next, you need to make a caftan, which is a large over-robe, out of a different color drapery casement. Measure the distance from your child's shoulder to his feet. Whatever the measurement is, double it to have enough material for the caftan. Have your child stand with his arms out from his sides like a scarecrow. Measure from elbow to elbow to get the width of material you will need to make the caftan. Using illustration 2 as a guide, cut a slit up the center for a center front opening. The top should be rounded to fit about the neck. When this is done the caftan is complete.

The headpiece is made from a large square of soft fabric. Safety pin two strings on one side of the material, each about 6 inches out from the center. (Illustration 3-A) As an added decoration, you may want to tie a piece of braided rope around the headpiece.

In assembling this costume have your child don the under-robe and then caftan. Tie a rope over the caftan to belt in the waist. (Illustration 4) Put the headpiece in place by tying the two strings behind your child's head and letting the material fall over, covering the strings. (Illustration 3-B) Slip on the sandals, and an extra piece of fabric can be folded and thrown over his shoulder to add an extra touch.

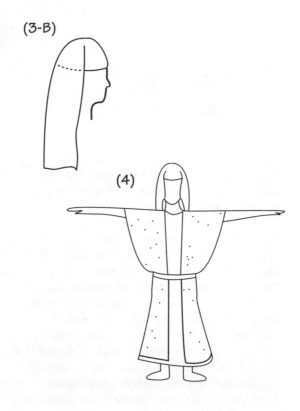

(3-B)

(4)

D

uring the last few weeks of December, schoolgirls are often asked to portray the Virgin Mary in Christmas nativity plays. Here is an easy method to create this costume.

MATERIALS NEEDED
* White fabric
* Blue fabric
* Cord
* White glue
* Sandals

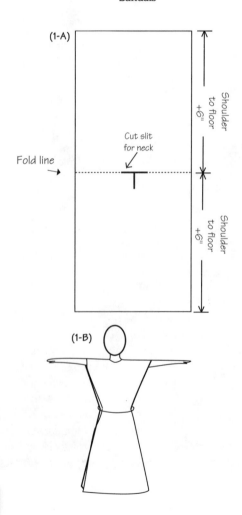

(1-A)

Shoulder to floor +6"

Cut slit for neck

Fold line →

Shoulder to floor +6"

(1-B)

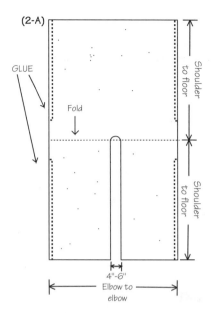

(2-A)

GLUE

Fold

Shoulder to floor

Shoulder to floor

4"-6"

Elbow to elbow

To make the Biblical girl's under-robe, we suggest that you use a soft white fabric. The under-robe is essentially a very full poncho. Measure the distance from your child's shoulder to her feet. Whatever the measurement is, double it and add 12 inches to get the length of material you will need to make the robe.

(2-B)

With the material folded in half lengthwise, cut a slit in the center just large enough through which to fit the head. (Illustration 1-A) This is worn like a poncho but corded in at the waist. Any extra material in length is bloused over the cord. (Illustration 1-B)

Next, you will need to make a caftan, which is a large over-robe, out of soft blue material. Measure the distance from your child's shoulder to her feet. Whatever the measurement is, double it to have enough material for the caftan. Have your child stand with her arms out from her sides like a scarecrow. Measure from elbow to elbow to get the width of material you will need to make the caftan. Using illustration 2-A as a guide, cut out a 4- to 6-inch section halfway up the center for a center front opening. The top should be rounded to fit about the neck. When this is done, fold in half lengthwise and glue the sides shut leaving an opening to put the arms through. (Illustration 2-B)

To make a headpiece, use a very large piece of soft white material. In length it should measure twice the distance of that from head to floor. Safety pin two strings on one side of the material. They should be pinned about 6 inches on either side of the center point. (Illustration 3-A)

In assembling this costume, have your child first don the white under-robe corded and bloused at the waist. Then put on the blue caftan. Next tie the headpiece in place allowing the material to fall down her back and over her shoulders. (Illustration 3-B) The longer the headpiece the more angelic the Mary will appear. As an added decoration, a piece of braided fabric can be tied about the headpiece.

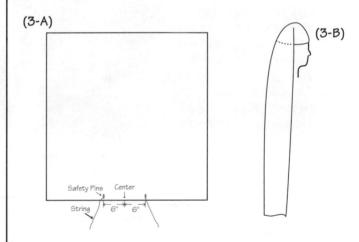

(3-A)

Safety Pins   Center

String   6"   6"

(3-B)

THREE WISE MEN

The Wise Men are three familiar figures in every Christmas pageant. Making these costumes, however, often proves to be a nightmare for many parents and teachers. Our easy-to-follow directions and illustrations should eliminate all your headaches.

MATERIALS NEEDED
* Soft flowing materials (for under-robes)
* Brocades & lamés (for over-robes & tabards)
* Imitation leopard skin material (for the front part of Balthazar's tabard)
* Gold vinyl
* Dark gold-, black-, and amber-colored marking pens
* White crepe paper
* Sandals
* White glue
* Hot glue gun
* Imitation jewels
* Gold trim
* Plastic bleach bottles
* Contact cement
* Cardboard box and 2 cans of hair spray (for the 3 gifts)
* Gold braid

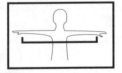

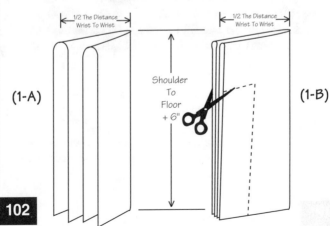

(1-A)   (1-B)

1/2 The Distance Wrist To Wrist

Shoulder To Floor + 6"

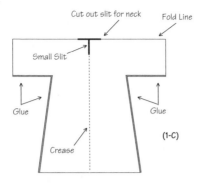

Cut out slit for neck   Fold Line

Small Slit

Glue   Glue

(1-C)

Crease

All three kings wear sandals and the same type of under-robe. Other than that, each costume is different. Since the under-robe is the basis for all three costumes, we'll start off by explaining how to make this garment.

Measure the distance from your child's shoulder to his feet. Whatever the measurement is, double it and add 12 inches to get the length of material you will need to make the under-robe. Have your child stand with his arms out from his sides like a scarecrow. Measure from wrist to wrist to get the width of material you will need to make the under-robe.

Fold the material in half, first lengthwise and then again widthwise. (Illustration 1-A) Cut a piece out of the lower free corners as shown in illustration 1-B. Unfold the material widthwise revealing a bell-shaped pattern. (Illustration 1-C) Make an opening for the head by cutting a slit in the center lengthwise fold. Also make a slit down the center front crease. It is always best not to make the openings too big. Start small and increase it gradually until your child can fit his head in easily. Glue the side seams shut by applying white glue about 1/2 inch away from the edge of the fabric and then press the two pieces of material together with your fingers. When the glue has dried, turn the robe inside out to hide the seams.

Now that we have completed the under-robe, which will be worn by all three characters, we will concentrate on the individual costumes.

The first king is Caspar. In addition to sandals and the basic under-robe, Caspar will need a caftan which is a black over-robe. To make this, measure the distance from your child's shoulder to his feet. Whatever the measurement is, double it to get the length of material you will need to make the caftan. Have your child stand with his arms out from his sides like a scarecrow. Measure from elbow to elbow to get the width of material you will need to make the caftan.

Using illustration 2-A as a guide, cut out a 4- to 6-inch section halfway up the center for a center front opening. The top should be rounded to fit about the neck. Glue gold trim along the sides and around the center front opening.

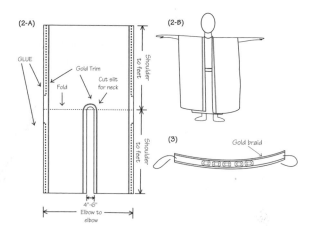

When this is done, fold the material in half lengthwise and glue the sides shut leaving an opening to put the arms through. (Illustration 2-B)

The caftan is worn over the under-robe which is sashed in about the waist with a 3-inch wide belt made from a piece of gold vinyl. For added decorations, use hot glue to secure fancy gold braids and imitation jewels to the vinyl. (Illustration 3) To secure the belt around the waist, punch holes in the back and lace shut with a shoelace.

Caspar's outfit also needs a collar which will be made of gold vinyl. To make the collar, fold the gold vinyl into quarters. Using a piece of string as a guide, mark off a quarter of a circle with a radius about 2 inches. This will fit around the child's neck. (Remember, the circumference of a circle is equal to 2 x 3.14 x the radius. So, if your child's neck measures 12 1/2 inches, then the radius of the circle will be 12.50 / 6.28 or about 2 inches). Measure now the distance between your child's neck and his shoulder. Whatever the distance is add 1 inch and draw another 1/4 circle. (Illustration 4-A) Cut out the two arcs and along one fold. (Illustration 4-B) You will now have the collar piece. Attach some gold braid and imitation jewels onto the collar with hot glue. Decorate with dark gold-, black-, and amber-colored marking pens. To secure the collar around the neck, safety pin in place.

(4-A)

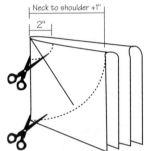

Neck to shoulder +1"

2"

(4-B)

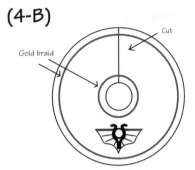

Cut

Gold braid

Caspar also gets a crown which is worn over a large square of soft material. The cloth headpiece is a 4-foot square. The material is placed on the child's head with one corner folded underneath. (Illustration 5) The longest part of the cloth is left to hang down toward the back. The cloth is secured by the crown, which is made from the plastic cut from a thoroughly washed bleach bottle. (Illustration 6) Use contact cement to attach gold vinyl to the plastic. For added decorations, hot glue gold braids and imitation jewels to the vinyl.

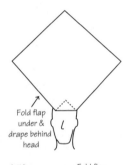

Fold flap under & drape behind head

(5)

Fold flap under

(6)

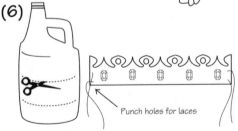

Punch holes for laces

The second king is Melchior. You will notice that besides sandals and the basic under-robe, there are some similarities between Melchior's outfit and Caspar's costume. Melchior's over-robe is made similar to Caspar's over-robe except the side seams are not closed and the shoulders are gathered by simply tying them with two small cords or laces. (Illustration 7)

To make Melchior's wig and beard, use white crepe paper. Cut the paper in strips about 1 foot wide and 2 inches longer than the length that you want the wig and beard to be when finished. Now cut these strips vertically into 1-inch-wide strips, leaving an uncut border at the top about 1 inch wide. (Illustration 8-A)

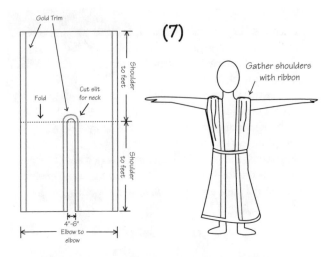

(7)

Gold Trim

Fold

Cut slit for neck

Shoulder to feet

Shoulder to feet

4"-6"
Elbow to elbow

Gather shoulders with ribbon

You can now curl the strips by holding one of the 1-inch strips between the thumb and first finger of the left hand just below the 1-inch border. Holding a pencil between the thumb and first finger of the right hand, place the paper strip between the thumb and the pencil. By gently pulling the pencil toward you and applying pressure on the pencil with the thumb you will cause the paper to curl. (Illustration 8-B) By applying more pressure with the thumb the curl can be made tighter.

Three strips of curls can now be glued together one on top of the other at the 1-inch border. (Illustration 8-C) The bottom layer should have loose curls while the curls on each additional layer should become progressively tighter. These sets of curls may be attached to a painter's cap,

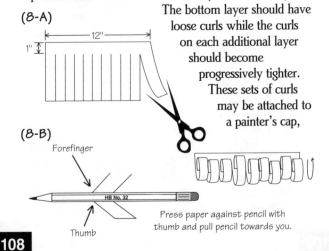

(8-A)

12"

1"

(8-B)

Forefinger

HB No. 32

Thumb

Press paper against pencil with thumb and pull pencil towards you.

which has had it's brim removed, to form a wig. A piece of elastic or cloth tape can be attached to a set of curls to form the beard. This may be fastened under the chin and tied over the top of the head.

Melchior's crown is made in the same way as Caspar's crown but it has a different design.

Melchior also wears a belt with a hangdown panel around his waist. This too is cut from gold vinyl. For added decorations, add gold braids and imitation jewels. (Illustration 9) To secure the belt and panel around the waist, punch holes in the back and lace shut with a shoelace.

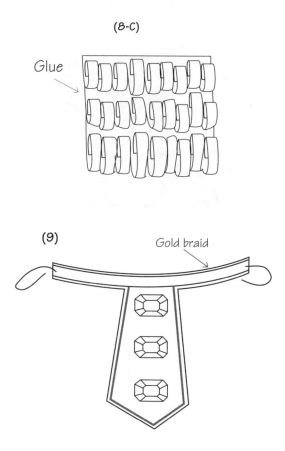

(8-C)

Glue

(9)

Gold braid

The third king is Balthazar. As with the other two kings, Balthazar will wear sandals and the basic under-robe. To this we will add a modified tabard. (Illustration 10) The length of the front part of the tabard should measure the distance from your child's shoulder to the floor. The width should measure from shoulder to shoulder. The back part of the tabard should be longer than shoulder to floor, to give it a slight train, and it should be wider at the bottom. The front part and the back part can be made from two different pieces of material which can be laced at the shoulders.

Balthazar gets a collar which is made similar to the one we made for Caspar. He also gets a belt and panel. (Illustration 11) Attach some gold braid and imitation jewels onto the panel with hot glue. Decorate the gold vinyl with dark gold-, black-, and amber-colored marking pens. Attach some gold braid and imitation gem stones onto the panel with glue. To secure the belt and panel around the waist, punch holes in the back and lace shut with a shoelace.

Balthazar, like Melchior, wears a crown with a cloth headpiece. (Illustration 12)

The Three Wise Men are known for carrying gifts. To

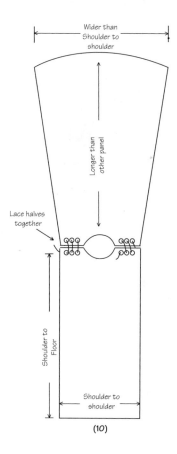

(10)

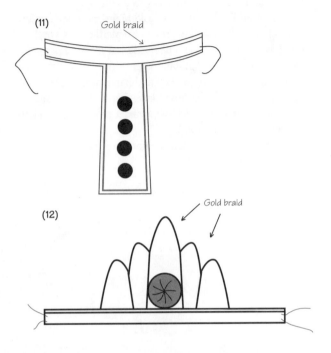

(11) Gold braid

(12) Gold braid

make these gifts, all you need is a small cardboard box and two empty aerosol cans. Tape the box shut with masking tape, and remove the tops and nozzles from the cans of hair spray. Next, spray the box and two cans with gold paint. After the paint has dried, glue gold trim around the box as well as the two cans. Glue imitation jewels and gold braid onto the objects to give the appearance that these are royal gifts.

ELF

113

ften more than one elf is needed for school Christmas shows. Red and green color combinations can offer enough variety to costume enough elves to handle Santa's workshop.

MATERIALS NEEDED
* Red and green felt
* White glue
* Red or green tights
* A fancy rope, cord or belt
* Red shoelaces or gold cord
* Red or green leotard or sweater
* Black vinyl, cardboard and aluminum foil
(for shoe buckles)

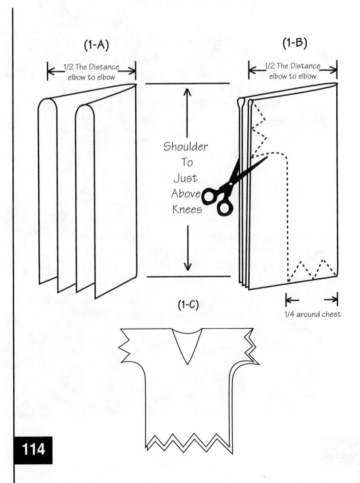

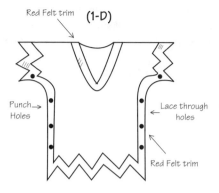

Red Felt trim (1-D)

Punch → Holes

Lace through ← holes

Red Felt trim

    Measure the distance from your child's shoulder to
above his knees. Whatever the measurement is, double it to
get the length of material you will need to make the tunic.
Have your child stand with his arms out from his sides like a
scarecrow. Measure from elbow to elbow to get the width
of the material you will need to make the tunic.

    Fold the green felt in half, first lengthwise and then
again widthwise. (Illustration 1-A) Using illustration 1-B as a
guide, cut out the main part of the tunic. Now unfold the
material widthwise to reveal a T-shaped pattern.
(Illustration 1-C) Next, you must cut an opening for the
head. In the center front, cut out a "V" large enough just to
get the head through. The tunic will fit better if you also
slightly round the back where the neck is. Enhance the
outfit by adding trim. (Illustration 1-D) Cut out pieces of red
felt for trim and use white glue to secure it across the
bottom, around the sleeves and around the neckline. Punch
holes along the sides and lace shut with red shoelaces or
gold cord.

Following illustration 2, cut out the hood. After you have cut your fabric to size, glue the appropriate edges together with white glue and give it ample time to dry. Turn the piece inside out to hide the seams and add red felt trim around the edges using glue.

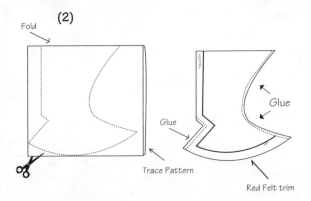

(2)

Fold

Glue

Glue

Trace Pattern

Red Felt trim

To assemble, have your youngster put on a pair of red or green tights. Next, have him slip on either a red or green leotard or sweater. The tunic comes next only to be followed by the hood. A fancy rope, cord or belt can be worn around the waist. Any type of shoes will do providing you add that magical touch. Cut out two pieces of cardboard to resemble big shoe buckles and cover them with aluminum foil. Insert a piece of black felt between each buckle and secure the buckles to the shoes with either elastic or string. (Illustration 3)

(3)

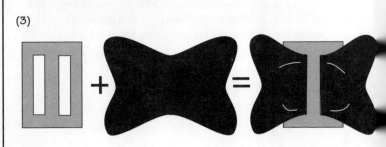

Over the years this costume has become quite popular. Part of its success lies in the fact that it is both novel and easy to make. If your child ever needs a quick, easy costume, this outfit will prove its worth.

MATERIALS NEEDED
* Leotard and tights (long johns will work in a pinch)
* Green fabric dye
* Blue 9-inch balloons
* Safety pins
* String
* Green crepe paper (or green felt or foam rubber)

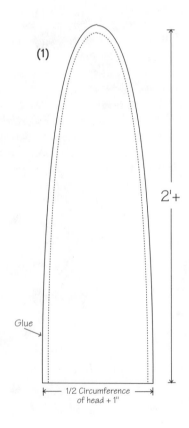

(1)

2'+

Glue

1/2 Circumference
of head + 1"

Begin by dying your child's leotard and tights with green fabric dye. This can be done in a bucket with hot water if you don't want to use your washing machine. If you use your washing machine be sure to run through an extra load of old clothes after you dye to clean out any residue of green dye left in the machine. If you dye in a bucket be sure to rinse the leotard and tights thoroughly with cold water before drying. When the clothes have dried, attach safety pins at even intervals over the torso.

The finishing touches can now be added less than 30 minutes before your child leaves the house. Inflate the balloons and tie long pieces of string around their stems. The balloons don't have to be inflated the same size. It looks best to have a variation. To attach the balloons to the costume, thread the strings through the safety pins and tie them in place. Be sure to cut off the excess string.

Large leaves can be cut from green crepe paper, foam rubber painted green or green felt and attached to the costume with tape or safety pins.

A large elf-like hat, resembling a stem, can be made from felt stuffed with newspapers as follows: Cut two pieces of felt following illustration 1. Using white glue, glue the edges as shown and, when dry, turn inside out to hide the seams. To give the hat some shape, stuff it with a little newspaper.

In school plays, children are often required to be costumed as flowers. Perhaps the most challenging task for any parent is to outfit the entire field of poppies in *The Wizard of Oz*. Flower costumes look simple, but their construction often confuses the costumer. Here is a simple costuming technique which dates as far back as the Romans.

MATERIALS NEEDED:
* A roll of round reed, size 10
* Red fabric dye
* White glue
* Red nylon chiffon (or red crystal sheer)
* Green tights and leotard
* Green felt

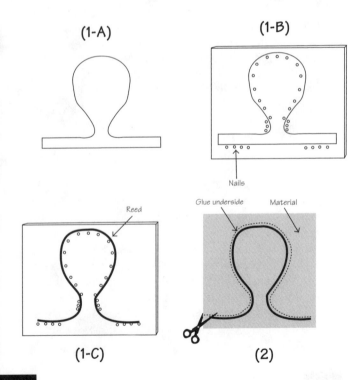

(1-A)

(1-B)

Nails

Reed

Glue underside   Material

(1-C)

(2)

While looking at the petals of a flower, cut out a paper pattern of an oversized petal. The outline of the pattern should be no longer than the lengths of your reed, and the base of the pattern needs to begin and end at 180 degrees. (Illustration 1-A) Lay the pattern on a thick wooden board and hammer long finishing nails around the pattern. (Illustration 1-B) The paper pattern can now be thrown away.

The reed needs to be placed around the nails, but to make it pliable it must first be soaked in hot water. Fill your bathtub, sanitary tub, or for that matter a large bucket, with very hot water (the hotter the better) and submerge the reed. Leave the reed in the receptacle until it becomes flexible. (Depending on how hot you are able to keep the water, this will take at least 15 minutes.) At this stage, you may want to add red fabric dye to the water. This will stain the reed and eliminate you having to paint it afterwards. It may, however, also stain your bathtub. So if you are adding the dye you may wish to restrict yourself to the use of the stationary tub or a bucket.

Wrap the now pliable reed around the nail board and cut it off to size. (Illustration 1-C) Repeat this process until you have enough petal frames for your flower. The reed should remain on the nail board for at least an entire day in order to give it ample time to dry. Once dry, the reed will become stiff and retain the shape of the original pattern.

In addition to the petal frames, you will also need a round piece of reed onto which you will attach all the petals. To make this piece, again prepare the reed by soaking. The only difference is that instead of wrapping the reed around the nail board, you will leave the piece inside an empty bucket to dry. When the reed has finally dried, remove the coiled piece and form a circle that is large enough to fit loosely over the child's head. Cut the piece to size and wrap the overlapped ends together with duct tape.

The next step involves attaching the material to the petal frames. When buying your fabric, you can either use red crystal sheer or red nylon chiffon. Coat one entire side of a petal frame with white glue. While the glue is still tacky, lay it down onto the fabric and press firmly in place. Once it has dried, cut off the excess fabric around the edges. (Illustration 2)

The petals now need to be attached individually to the round circular piece of reed. To do this, secure the petals to the ring by using duct tape. (Illustration 3) Glue green felt leaves about the base to hide the duct tape.

Your child could, of course, just wear this huge flower over green tights and a leotard, and the costume would look just fine. If, however, you would like to add a finishing touch, make two smaller flowers, using the techniques you were just taught, and place one of the smaller flowers on each hand. Hold these in place with elastic.

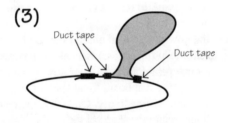

(3)

Duct tape

Duct tape

ere is a costume with which you can have a barrel of fun.

Foam rubber is a wonderful product that can be used to construct a multitude of unusual costumes. Once you master the basic techniques, you can make oversized fruits, vegetables, or other larger-than-life products.

(1-A)

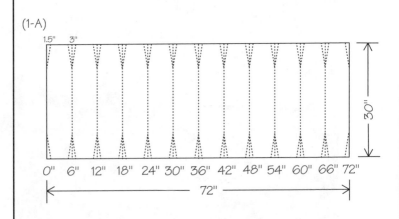

The barrel requires a rectangular piece of 1-inch foam rubber measuring 30 inches by 72 inches which will be glued together along the 30-inch sides to form a cylinder and darted in at the top and bottom to give it a barrel shape.

To do this one must begin by marking every 6 inches along both of the 72-inch sides. Using the mark as the center of the base, draw an isosceles triangle, the base of which should measure 3 inches and the height 10 inches. At the ends, however, draw a right triangle the base of which should measure only 1 1/2 inches and the height 10 inches. (Illustration 1A) Using a butcher knife, cut out the triangles.

With a 1-inch paint brush, brush contact cement along the edges of the foam. Allow this to dry just enough that it is no longer wet to the touch. Don't try to glue the edges while they are still wet. When the glue is dry to the touch, glue the 30-inch sides together to form a cylinder and then dart in the top and bottom.

Around the top and the bottom of the barrel, glue a 1 1/2 inch strip of foam rubber for rims. Also glue 2 additional strips 10 inches from the top and 10 inches from the bottom. (Illustration 1B)

Now all one needs to do is paint the foam rubber to look like a barrel. Use the darts as guidelines for the stays. A couple of painted knot holes add to the realism. The barrel can be held in place with a pair of clip-on suspenders or two pieces of rope.

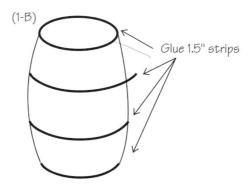

(1-B)

Glue 1.5" strips

hildren think there is something magical about making a costume out of regular cardboard boxes. Box costumes are relatively easy to make and they're inexpensive.

Here are a few good pointers to consider when making a box costume. After finding a suitably sized and shaped box, cut out holes to allow free movement of the head, arms and legs. Any necessary additions to the box can be made with extra pieces of cardboard or plastic bottles and lids. Attach these items with either white glue, staples or tape. Cover the box as required with paint, aluminum foil, contact paper, crepe paper or felt.

Here are three of the more popular types of costumes that can be made from regular cardboard boxes, a few incidental items and your imagination:

Die

Cut a hole in the top of a box that is large enough to get your child's head through. Next, cut two smaller holes in the sides for the arms. Once inside, the square box should be long enough to extend from the neck to above your youngster's knees. Use white and black felt to cover the box. If you don't have felt you may use white latex paint and a roller. After the paint has thoroughly dried, use black paint to make spots on the sides of the box. The spots should be the same size as the three cut-out holes. Although the opposite sides of a die always add up to 7, it is best to put a 5 on one side and a 3 on the opposite side so the arms can come out of the black spots. For undergarments, wear a black leotard and tights.

Television

Cut the bottom from a large rectangular shaped box. Next, cut out a small square hole for the face and cover the inside with transparent plastic, held in place by tape. Cover the entire box with wood grain contact paper or paint. Glue on bottle caps and lids for knobs. If possible, make a rabbit ear's antenna out of assorted hardware items and attach to the top of the box costume.

Robot

Since the 1950s, boys have been fascinated with building robot costumes out of boxes. In addition to needing several suitably sized boxes, you will also need a quantity of aluminum foil. The boxes should be covered with the foil and secured in place with tape. Use bottle tops and lids to create the illusion of robot dials and control switches. Cover your child's old shirt and a pair of pants with aluminum foil. Shoes could be covered with foil or, better yet, have your son wear his black rain boots. Black rubber gloves make a good substitute for the robot's hands.

Robin Hood, the beloved rogue of Sherwood Forest, was a legendary archer known for his courtesy and courage. Over the years he has been the subject of numerous books and films, and is still a popular folk hero among youngsters and adults alike.

MATERIALS NEEDED:

* Two pieces of non-woven, heavy material preferably felt. Fabrics should be contrasting rustic colors such as brown and forest green.
* Rawhide, or black or brown shoelaces (for lacings)
* White glue
* Tights
* Black vinyl (for wrist bands)
* Pair of men's woolly socks (either brown or green)
* Toy bow and arrow
* Belt
* A feather

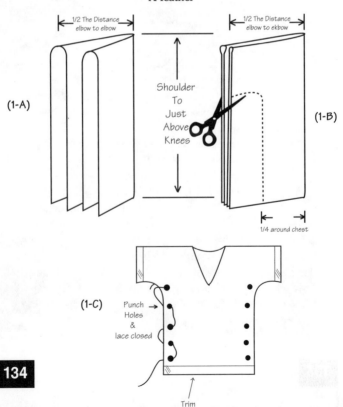

(1-A)

(1-B)

1/2 The Distance elbow to elbow

1/2 The Distance elbow to ekbow

Shoulder To Just Above Knees

1/4 around chest

(1-C)

Punch Holes & lace closed

Trim

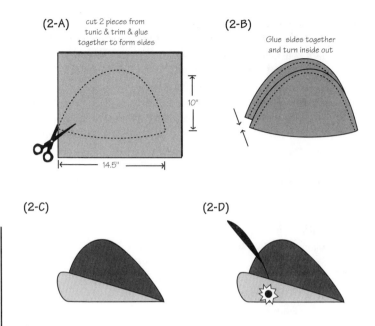

(2-A) cut 2 pieces from tunic & trim & glue together to form sides

10"

14.5"

(2-B) Glue sides together and turn inside out

(2-C)

(2-D)

Measure the distance from your child's shoulder to above his knees. Whatever the measurement is, double it to get the length of material you will need to make the tunic. Have your child stand with his arms out from his sides like a scarecrow. Measure from elbow to elbow to get the width of material you will need to make the tunic.

Fold the material in half, first lengthwise and then again widthwise. (Illustration 1-A) Using illustration 1-B as a guide, cut out the main part of the tunic. Now unfold the material widthwise to reveal a T-shaped pattern. (Illustration 1-C) Next, you must cut an opening for the head. In the center front, cut out a "V" large enough just to get the head through. The tunic will fit better if you slightly round the back where the neck is. Enhance the outfit by adding trim. Cut out pieces of a contrasting material for trim and use white glue to secure it across the bottom, around the sleeves and around the neckline. Punch holes along the sides and lace shut with rawhide, or black or brown shoelaces.

The hat is easily made out of the same material as the tunic and the tunic trim. Following illustration 2-A cut two pieces out of the material used for the tunic and 2 pieces out of the material used for the tunic trim. Glue the trim pieces to each one of the other pieces. Following illustration 2-B, glue these two pieces together with the trim sides inside. Turn one end up to get the characteristic shape. (Illustration 2-C) Decorate the hat as shown in illustration 2-D.

Following illustration 3, cut out two pieces of black vinyl that will fit comfortably around your son's wrists. Holes should be punched into each side of the vinyl and then these cuffs should be laced around your child's wrists by using either rawhide or black or brown shoelaces.

(3)

For the legs, wear green tights. If the weather is cold, an appropriate color turtleneck sweater makes a perfect under-tunic. Wear regular shoes and pull a large pair of brown or green woolly socks over the shoes to make booties. A wide leather belt should be worn. Use a man's belt and just add extra holes for fit. Don't cut off the excess length, but wrap it about as can be seen in the photograph.

Top off your costume with a toy bow-and-arrow set, and you're ready to roam Sherwood Forest.

FRIAR TUCK

137

ere is Robin Hood's trustworthy companion, the legendary Friar Tuck. This costume can also double for a monk.

MATERIALS NEEDED
* Dark brown material (for robe and cowl)
* Light brown material (for tabard)
* White glue
* Sandals
* Thick white rope
* Down jacket

Measure the distance from your child's shoulder to his feet. Whatever the measurement is, double it and add 12 inches to get the length of material you will need to make the monk's robe. Have your child stand with his arms out from his sides like a scarecrow. Measure from wrist to wrist to get the width of material you will need to make the robe. Fold the material in half, first lengthwise and then again widthwise. (Illustration 1-A) Using illustration 1-B as a guide, cut a piece out of the lower free corners. Unfold the material widthwise revealing a bell-shaped pattern. (Illustration 1-C)

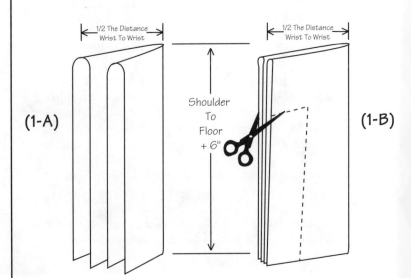

(1-A)

1/2 The Distance
Wrist To Wrist

1/2 The Distance
Wrist To Wrist

Shoulder
To
Floor
+ 6"

(1-B)

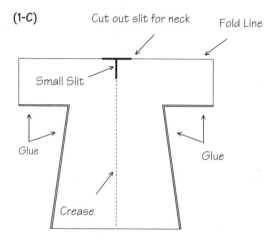

(1-C)

Cut out slit for neck

Fold Line

Small Slit

Glue

Glue

Crease

Make an opening for the head by cutting a small slit in the center of the lengthwise fold. Also make a small slit down the center front crease for the neck. It is best not to make these openings too big. Start small and increase it gradually until your child can fit his head in easily.

Glue the appropriate side seams shut by applying white glue about 1/2 inch away from the edge of the fabric and then press the two pieces of material together with your fingers. When the glue has dried, turn the robe inside out.

Using the light brown material, make a tabard. A tabard is simply a rectangular piece of material. The width is the same as the distance between the shoulders and the length is twice the distance as measured from shoulder to floor. A "T" shape is cut in the center for the head. (Illustration 2)

Follow illustration 3 to make a monk's cowl. After you have cut your fabric to size, glue the appropriate edges together with white glue and give it ample time to dry. Turn the hood inside out when you are finished.

Since Friar Tuck was known for his rotund figure, it is suitable to wear a down jacket for padding under the robe.

This will fill out the costume to the right proportions.
Wearing the robe and tabard over the down jacket, tie a
thick white cord around his waist, blousing the robe over
the rope. Fold back the excess material on the sleeves to
form large cuffs. Place the cowl over your child's head,
and he's ready to either stroll through Sherwood Forest or
join a monastery.

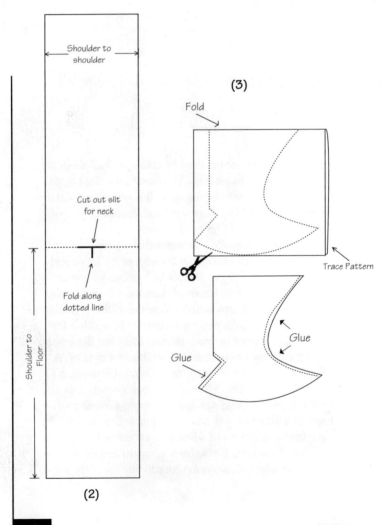

sk anyone to name the greatest detective in the world and the odds are he'll say, "Sherlock Holmes." Thanks to his numerous appearances on television and in movies, plays, and books, this fictional character is as popular today as ever before.

MATERIALS NEEDED
* Dark felt
* White glue
* Dark suit or dark colored coat and pants
* Dark shoes
* White shirt
* Four-in-hand tie
* Two matching baseball caps (or painter's caps)
* Corsage pin
* Pipe and magnifying glass

For the most part, this outfit is made from everyday clothes. Although a dark suit is ideal for this costume, a dark coat and pair of pants will work equally as well. Once your child is properly dressed, and his necktie is in place, turn his shirt collar up to create the illusion of a wing-collared shirt. To transform a regular necktie into a cravat, use a corsage pin as a pearl stickpin.

A deerstalker's cap can be created without sewing by using two peaked caps. Baseball or company caps without logo designs are the perfect substitute for a detective's hat. If you're in a pinch, white painter's caps will also do the job, but you'll have to dye them a dark color. To assemble your deerstalker's hat, just place one of the caps backwards on your son's head and then nest the other cap over in the normal position. Using a material resembling that of the baseball caps, cut two earflaps and glue to the sides facing

(1)

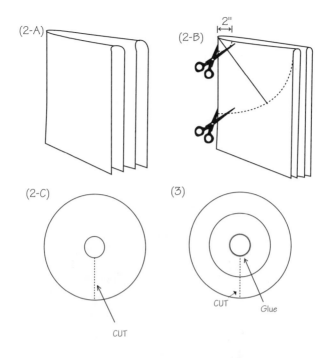

(2-A)

(2-B) 2"

(2-C)

CUT

(3)

CUT   Glue

up. Attach a string to the free end of each flap with glue and tie above the hat. (Illustration 1)

To make an inverness cape, you'll need to make two capes, a long one (for the cape) and a shorter one (for the capelet). To make a cape, use a full circle. This is simply done by folding the material into quarters. (Illustration 2-A) By using a piece of string as a guide, mark off a quarter circle with a radius about 2 inches and then another with a much larger radius which will be the length of your cape. (Illustration 2-B) Cut out the circles and then cut along one of the radii for an opening. (Illustration 2-C)

To make the capelet, do exactly as you did for the cape but this time use a smaller radius. The cape and capelet should form concentric circles. Put the capelet on top of the cape and fasten them together by gluing along the neck holes. (Illustration 3) The cape and capelet can be secured around the neck with a safety pin.

A pipe and magnifying glass make wonderful hand props, and complete the character.

King Arthur's personal wizard, Merlin, has become the most famous of all magicians. Just follow some simple instructions and you can create, just like magic, your own wizard's outfit.

MATERIALS NEEDED
* Black felt
* White glue
* Gold vinyl
* A fancy colored rope or cord (preferably gold)
* Poster board
* Play eyeglasses (optional)
* White crepe paper

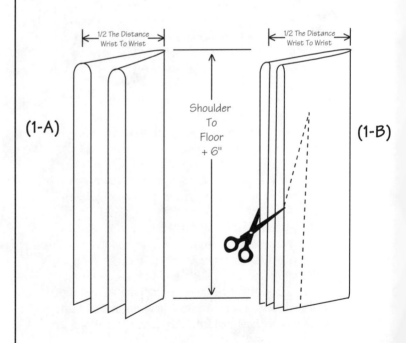

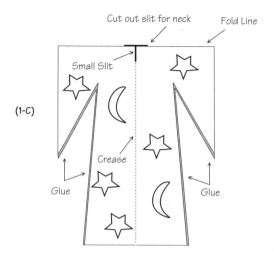

(1-C)

Cut out slit for neck   Fold Line

Small Slit

Crease

Glue   Glue

Measure the distance from your child's shoulder to his feet. Whatever the measurement is, double it and add 12 inches to get the length of material you will need to make the robe. Next, have your child stand with his arms out from his sides like a scarecrow. Measure from wrist to wrist to get the width of material you will need to make the robe.

To make the robe, fold the material in half first lengthwise and then again widthwise. (Illustration 1-A)

Following illustration 1-B, cut a piece out of the lower free corners. Unfold the material widthwise revealing a bell shaped pattern. (Illustration 1-C) You will now need to make an opening for the head. Cut a small slit in the center of the lengthwise fold. Next, cut a small slit down the center front crease. Remember it is always best not to make the openings too big.

Using white glue, glue the edges by applying it about 1/2 inch away from the edge of the fabric and then press the two pieces of material together with your fingers. When this has dried, turn the robe inside out to hide the seams. Cut some mystical symbols, such as crescent moons and stars, out of gold vinyl or some similar contrasting material that doesn't fray, such as gold felt. Glue these to the robe.

Slip the robe on and draw it in around the waist with a gold cord. Draw up any excess length and blouse over the cord. If the sleeves are too long don't cut them off. Instead, pleat them along the arm to give plenty of fullness. This can be done first with pins to get the desired length. Then glue these pleats in place and remove the pins.

The magician's hat can be made out of poster board or a flexible cardboard. Roll a piece of it into a cone, staple it in place and trim the bottom edge to make it even. Cover the poster board with the same material that was used to make the robe and glue on some stars. A piece of elastic may be attached by stapling or punching holes in the rim of the hat on either side

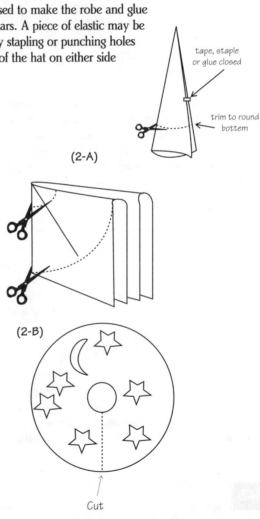

tape, staple
or glue closed

trim to round
bottom

(2-A)

(2-B)

Cut

and tying knots to secure it. The elastic should be long enough to fit comfortably under the chin, but tight enough to keep the hat in place.

To make the capelet, use a full circle. This is simply done by folding the material into quarters. By using a piece of string as a guide, mark off a quarter circle. (Illustration 2-A) The size of your child will determine the radius of the circle. You will also need to cut out a small circle in the center for the neck. The radius of this will probably be about 2 inches. Cut the neck hole small at first and then trim until you have a good fit. You will also have to cut an opening in the circle. (Illustration 2-B) The capelet should also be decorated with the same symbols. Safety pin the capelet in place around the neck.

A wig and beard are necessary. To give the effect of hair, use white crepe paper. Cut the paper in strips about 12 inches wide and 2 inches longer than the length that you want the wig and beard to be when finished. Now cut these

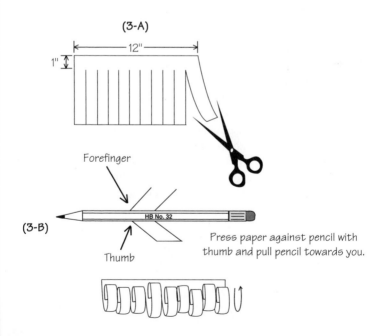

(3-A)

12"

1"

Forefinger

HB No. 32

(3-B)

Thumb

Press paper against pencil with thumb and pull pencil towards you.

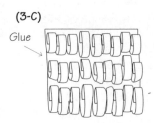

(3-C)

Glue

strips vertically into 1-inch wide strips leaving an uncut
border at the top about an inch wide. (Illustration 3-A)

You can now curl the strips by holding one of the 1-inch
strips between the thumb and first finger of the left hand just
below the 1-inch border. Holding a pencil between the
thumb and first finger of the right hand, place the paper strip
between the thumb and the pencil. By gently pulling the
pencil toward you and applying pressure on the pencil with
the thumb, you will cause the paper to curl. (Illustration 3-B)
By applying more pressure with the thumb the curl can be
made tighter.

Three strips of curls can now be glued together one on
top of the other at the 1-inch border. (Illustration 3-C) The
bottom layer should have loose curls while the curls on
each additional layer should become progressively tighter.
Sets of curls may be attached to the inside of the hat to
simulate hair. A piece of elastic or cloth tape can be attached
to a set of curls to form the beard. This may be fastened
under the chin and tied over the top of the head under the
hat, or tied to the frames of play eyeglasses.

This outfit is for the child who never wants to grow up.

MATERIALS NEEDED
* Green tights
* Green felt
* Rawhide or brown shoelaces
* Wide black leather belt
* Rubber dagger
* Pair of men's woolly socks (green)

(1-A)   (1-B)

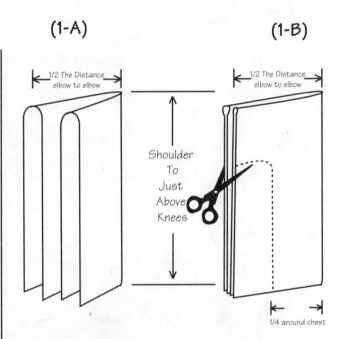

Measure the distance from you child's shoulder to above his knees. Whatever the measurement is, double it to get the length of material you will need to make the tunic. Next, have your child stand with his arms straight out from his sides like a scarecrow. Measure from elbow to elbow to get the width of material you will need to make the tunic.

Fold the material in half, first lengthwise and then again widthwise. (Illustration 1-A) Using illustration 1-B as a guide, cut out the main part of the tunic. Now unfold the material widthwise to reveal a T-shaped pattern. Following illustration 1-C, cut an opening for the head. In the center front, cut out a "V" large enough just to get the head through. The tunic will fit better if you also slightly round the hole at the back where the neck is. To give the costume an authentic look, jag the edges as shown in illustration 1-D. The tunic can be held together by punching holes along the sides and lacing it shut with either rawhide or brown shoelaces.

To assemble the outfit, put on the tights and then the tunic. Secure the tunic to the waist with a wide black leather belt. Next, place a rubber dagger inside the belt.

For footwear, pull a pair of men's green woolly socks over your child's shoes.

(1-C)

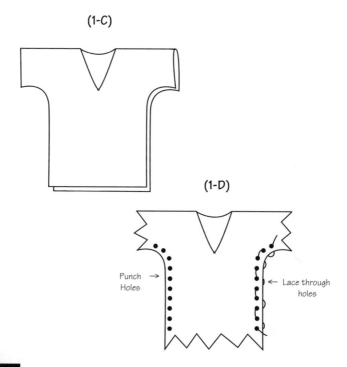

(1-D)

Punch → Holes

← Lace through holes

Julius Caesar was the conqueror of Gaul and dictator of Rome. He was not only a great general and statesman, but an orator, poet and historian. Coupled with Cleopatra, this costume will be a big success.

MATERIALS NEEDED
* White material
* Broach
* Aluminum wire
* Plastic, cloth or paper leaves
* Gold spray paint
* Gold glitter (optional)
* Sandals
* Thin wire, thread or florist tape

The tunic is essentially nothing more than a poncho that has been gathered at the shoulders with two pieces of ribbon tied through the neck hole. To make the tunic, take a piece of soft white material the width of which should be wider than your child's shoulder-to-shoulder measurement. The length when folded in half should measure the same as that from your child's shoulder to knee. Fold the material

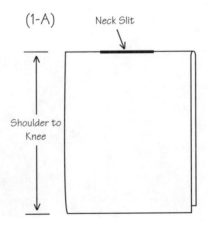

(1-A)   Neck Slit

Shoulder to Knee

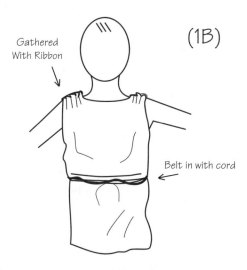

Gathered
With Ribbon

(1B)

Belt in with cord

lengthwise and put a slit in the center to put the head through. (Illustration 1-A) Next, simply take two ribbons or cords and gather the shoulders. Also take a cord and tie about the waist, and blouse the tunic over the cord. (Illustrations 1-B)

For the drape that hangs over the robe, take a piece of the same fabric used to make the robe and cut a large square, the sides of which should be the length of your child's shoulder-to-floor measurement. Taking two top

(2)

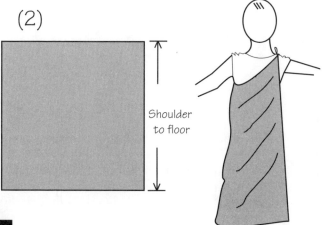

Shoulder to floor

corners, wrap the material around the body and tie the corners together over the left shoulder. (Illustration 2) If a broach is available, pin it on the knot.

Next, you will need to make a laurel wreath. (Illustration 3) Go to a craft store and buy some artificial green or gold leaves. Many times you will find that the leaves are already attached to wire in the form of a vine or just a spray of green foliage. This of course is your best buy. Then, all that is necessary is for you to bend the wire into the correct shape around the child's head.

If you already have some artificial leaves at home, attach them to a piece of aluminum wire with the aid of florist tape or merely by wrapping the stems on the wire with thread. White glue can be applied to the thread to help keep the leaves in place. When you have finished the wreath, you may paint it with gold spray paint. While the paint is still wet, dust the wreath with gold glitter. Make sure that the glitter sticks to the leaves and *does not* get into the child's eyes. While you're at it, you may also want to spray paint your child's sandals.

(3)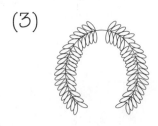

CLEOPATRA

leopatra, Queen of the Nile, is still regarded as one of the world's most beautiful women.

MATERIALS NEEDED
* Soft white material (for under-robe)
* Black and gold material (for over-robe)
* Gold vinyl
* White glue
* Hot glue gun
* Contact cement
* Dark gold-, black- and amber-colored marking pens
* Gold braid
* Fancy cord or rope
* Imitation jewels
* Plastic bleach bottle

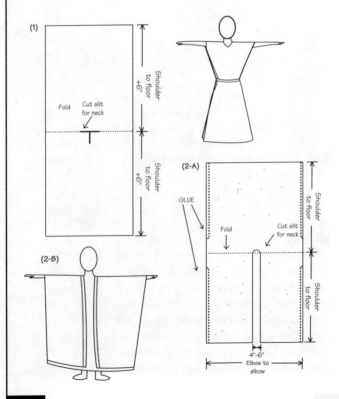

(3) Gold braid

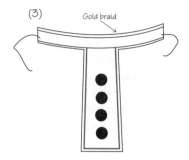

(4-A)

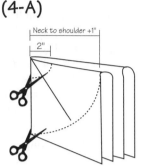

Neck to shoulder +1"

2"

To make Cleopatra's under-robe, we suggest you use a soft white fabric. The under-robe is **(4-B)** essentially a very full poncho. Measure the distance from your child's shoulder to her feet. Whatever the measurement is, double it and add 12 inches to get the length of material you will need to make the under-robe. Next, have your child stand with her arms out from her sides like a scarecrow. Measure from elbow to elbow to get the width of material you will need to make the under-robe. With the material folded in half lengthwise, cut a slit in the center just large enough to fit the head. This is worn like a poncho but corded in at the waist. Any excess material in length is bloused over the cord. (Illustration 1)

Cut

Gold braid

Next you will need to make a caftan, which is a large over-robe, out of black and gold material. Measure the distance from your child's shoulder to her feet. Whatever the measurement is, double it to have enough material for the caftan. Have your child stand with her arms out from her sides like a scarecrow. Measure from elbow to elbow to get the width of material you will need to make the caftan. Using illustration 2-A as a guide, cut out a 4- to 6-inch section halfway up the center for a center front opening. The top should be rounded to fit about the neck. When this is done, fold in half lengthwise and glue the sides shut leaving an opening to put the arms through. (Illustration 2-B)

Follow illustration 3 and make an Egyptian belt and panel out of gold vinyl. Attach some gold braid and imitation jewels onto the panel with hot glue. Decorate the panel with dark gold-, black-, and amber-colored marking pens. To secure the belt and panel around the waist, either safety pin in place or punch holes in the back and lace shut with fancy cord or ribbon.

Use gold vinyl to make a collar. Fold the material into quarters. Using a piece of string as a guide, mark off a quarter of a circle with a radius about 2 inches. This will fit around the child's neck. (Remember, the circumference of a circle is equal to 2 x 3.14 x the radius. If your child's neck measures 12 1/2 inches, then the radius of the circle will be 12.50 / 6.28 or about 2-inches) Measure the distance between your child's neck and her shoulder. Whatever the distance is, add 1 inch and draw another 1/4 circle. (Illustration 4-A) Cut out the two arcs and along one fold. (Illustration 4-B) You will now have the collar piece. Decorate the collar the same as you did with the Egyptian belt and panel. To secure the collar around the neck, safety pin in place.

The base of the headdress is made from the bottom of a thoroughly washed plastic bleach bottle that has been covered with contact cement and gold vinyl. The upright piece is made out of cardboard with a card support in the back. (Illustration 5) It is decorated with gold sequins and braid.

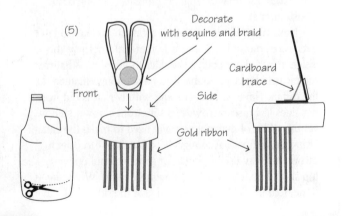

(5) Decorate with sequins and braid

Front   Side   Cardboard brace

Gold ribbon

Step right up folks and see this amazing human oddity. Gather in a little closer and we'll teach you how to create a great costume that will not only be the talk of the party, but made for very little money.

MATERIALS NEEDED:
* Pink- or flesh-colored body suit (or a leotard and tights)
* Multi-colored felt-tip marking pens (preferably indelible)
* Two-piece bathing suit or trunks
* Rubber snake
* Graphic art books (available at art supply stores)
* Wide bracelets

This costume is relatively easy to make providing you have a child who is fairly patient. If not, you may want to consider one of the other costumes in this chapter.

To make this classic sideshow attraction, have your child put on a pink- or flesh-colored body suit. Have the person being tattooed lie down and, using the images in the graphic art books as patterns, proceed to outline any familiar tattoo figures, e.g., skulls, anchors, eagles, etc. These books often have geometric patterns that can be repeated. Since tattooing an entire body is time consuming, use these repetitive patterns, which are much easier to do, to outline entire areas, such as the torso. Not only will this save time, it is an excellent way of blending in the edges of the body suit.

Using the other marking pens, fill in the designs with various colors. Wide bracelets may be worn on the wrists and ankles to help disguise the edges of the body suit or leotard and tights. Add a bathing suit, a pair of slippers and a fake rubber snake around the neck, and your little girl or boy is ready for the midway.

I f your son ever needs a quick costume and he has a dark suit in his closet, your prayers have been answered.

MATERIALS NEEDED
* Dark suit
* White felt
* Black felt
* White glue

Given a dark suit, all that remains for this costume is an imitation Roman collar and bib. This is made out of two pieces of black felt. The collar is a strip measuring 2 inches by 15 inches, on which a small white square of felt is glued in the center. (Illustration 1-A) The bib is cut according to illustration 1-B. The curved piece of the bib that will fit around the neck needs to be clipped so the collar can be glued to the bib. To assemble, glue the collar to the bib as shown in illustration 1-C.

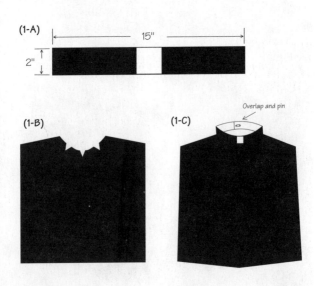

(1-A)

15"

2"

(1-B)

(1-C)

Overlap and pin

Over the years, nuns have been the subject of several feature-length films and at least one Broadway play. Here at last are simple directions on how to make a traditional nun's habit.

MATERIALS NEEDED
* Black fabric
* White glue
* White felt
* White string
* Thick white rope

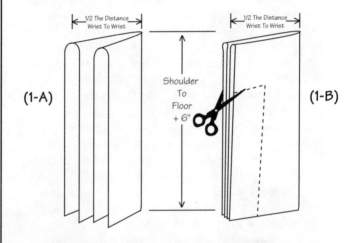

(1-A)   (1-B)

1/2 The Distance Wrist To Wrist

Shoulder To Floor + 6"

The nun's costume consists of a robe, tabard, belt, collar and headpiece. To make the robe, measure the distance from your child's shoulder to her feet. Whatever the measurement is, double it and add 12 inches to get the length of fabric you will need to make the robe. Have your child stand with her arms out from her sides like a scarecrow. Measure from wrist to wrist to get the width of material you will need to make the robe.

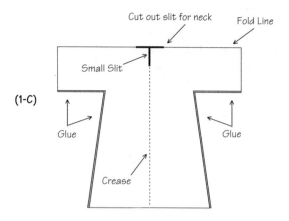

Cut out slit for neck

Fold Line

Small Slit

(1-C)

Glue

Glue

Crease

Fold the material in half, first lengthwise and then again widthwise. (Illustration 1-A) Cut a piece out of the lower free corners as shown in illustration 1-B. Unfold the material widthwise revealing a bell-shaped pattern. (Illustration 1-C) Make an opening for the head by cutting a slit in the center lengthwise fold. Also make a slit down the center front crease. It is always best not to make the openings too big. Start small and increase it gradually until your child can fit her head in easily. Glue the side seams shut by applying white glue about 1/2 inch away from the edge and then press the two pieces of material together with your fingers. When the glue has dried turn the robe inside out.

Using the same material as used for the robe, make a tabard. A tabard is simply a rectangular piece of material, the width of which is the same as the distance between the shoulders and the length of which is twice the distance as measured from the shoulder to the floor. A T-shaped slit is cut in the center for the head. (Illustration 2)

To make the collar, fold the felt into quarters. Using a piece of string as a guide, mark off a quarter of a circle with a radius about 2 inches. This will fit around her neck. (Remember, the circumference of a circle is equal to 2 x 3.14 x the radius. If your child's neck measures 12 1/2 inches then the radius of the circle will be 12.50 / 6.28 or about 2-inches) Measure the distance between your child's neck and her shoulder. Whatever that distance is add 2 inches and draw another 1/4 circle. (Illustration 3-A) Cut along the two arcs and along one radii for an opening and you will now have the nun's collar. (Illustration 3-B)

The nun's headpiece is very simple. It is just a 36-inch square of black material with two strings safety pinned on one side about 8 inches in from each side. To get the white edging, simply glue a piece of white felt between the two pins. (Illustration 4-A)

After donning the black robe, tie the white cord, which will act as a belt, around your child's waist. Blouse the excess length over the cord. Now slip the black tabard over the head. The white circle of felt is to be placed around the neck and just pinned in the back with a safety pin. To put the headpiece on properly, place the white felt on the forehead allowing the black material to drape over the back of the head. Secure the headpiece by tying the two strings around the child's head under the black material. (Illustration 4-B)

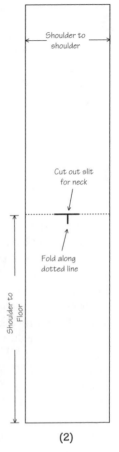

(2)

(3-A)

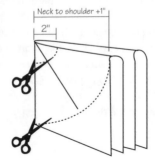

(3-B)

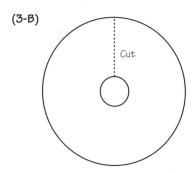

Cut

(4-A)

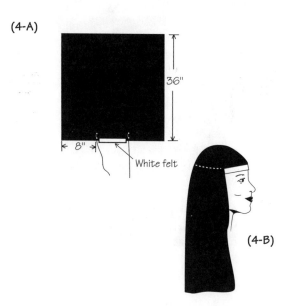

36"

8"

White felt

(4-B)

sing items that are readily available in your family's wardrobe, you can assemble this outfit in minutes.

MATERIALS NEEDED
* A man's solid-colored long-sleeve shirt
* Dark-colored pants
* Beret
* A strip of silky material
* Small piece of wood or cardboard
* A paint brush

We recommend your child wear a dark pair of pants with this costume. Black or brown dress pants are preferred over a pair of jeans. To this we add a man's long-sleeve shirt, from which its breast pocket has been removed, in a solid color such as blue, yellow, pink, etc. The oversized shirt will act as a smock on a small child.

Next, we need a large floppy tie. It is best to use a strip of solid color and silky material that contrasts with the shirt. Tie the material in a bow around the child's neck just as you would tie a shoelace.

Rather than make a beret, we suggest you simply buy one as they are very inexpensive. Berets can be found in a variety of stores such as costume, army surplus and vintage clothing shops.

To finish off this costume, your child will need a few artistic hand props, namely a paint brush and an artist's palette. The kidney-shaped palette can be made from either cardboard or wood. It should also have a hole in it so your child can put his thumb through it and hold the palette in place. Splatter a few colored paints on it for effect or, better yet, color in a few blotches with colored marking pens.

An extra touch is to add a small mustache, which can be drawn on with an eyebrow pencil.

Ahoy, buccaneers. Here is another one of those easy costumes you can make using items right out of your own wardrobe.

MATERIALS NEEDED
* White pants
* 1-inch masking tape
* Red and blue spray paint
* T-shirt
* White shirt
* Black shoes
* Bandanna or striped kerchief
* A long piece of red material 6 inches wide
* Black felt
* White glue
* Novelty sword
* Earring
* Eye patch

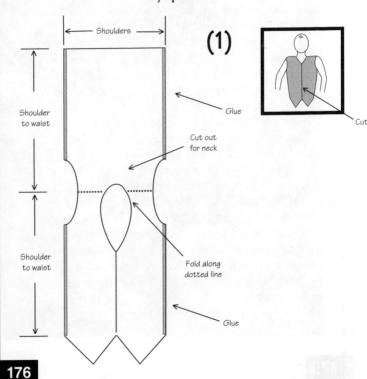

Shoulders

(1)

Shoulder to waist

Shoulder to waist

Glue

Cut out for neck

Fold along dotted line

Glue

Cut

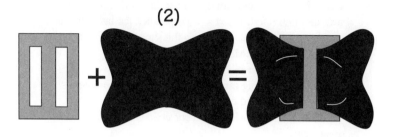

Lay a pair of white pants on a flat surface and stripe them vertically in measured intervals with 1-inch masking tape. Be sure to firmly press the masking tape to the pants. Dust them down with red spray paint. When the paint has dried and the tape is removed, you will have a pair of red-and-white striped pirate pants. Cut the pants below the knee to give them a tattered look.

Next, you will need to stripe your child's T-shirt. Follow the same procedure that was used in striping the pants. The only difference is that this time you will make horizontal stripes by using blue spray paint. After your child has put on his striped shirt, a white shirt should be worn over top. If the shirt is long sleeved, roll them up and then tie the shirt in a knot around the waist. For a sash, use a piece of contrasting material that is 6 inches wide and long enough to be wrapped around the waist at least twice and tied.

A vest, which may be considered optional, can easily be made from black felt. The width of the vest should be roughly the distance between the two shoulders, while the overall length should be twice the distance as measured from your child's shoulder to his waist. Following illustration 1, cut the vest and secure the appropriate edges with white glue. When the glue has dried, turn the vest inside out to hide the seams.

For footwear, your child should wear his regular black shoes. Make shoe buckles out of cardboard and cover them with aluminum foil. Insert a piece of black felt between each buckle and secure the buckles to the shoes with either elastic or string. (Illustration 2)

Use a triangular piece of material for a head scarf. A novelty sword, a big earring and an eye patch complete the costume.

With a little imagination, your child is ready to sail the seven seas.

he pirate girl costume is a lesson in simplicity.

MATERIALS NEEDED
* White blouse
* Black shorts or black skirt
* A long piece of red material 6 inches wide
* Black felt
* White glue
* Bandanna or striped kerchief (for head scarf)
* Novelty sword

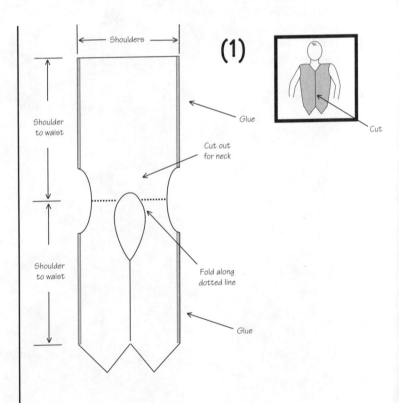

For the pirate girl costume, a white blouse is required. Your child will also need either black shorts or a black skirt tattered at the bottom.

A vest, which may be considered optional, can easily be made from black felt. The width of the vest should be roughly the distance between the two shoulders, while the overall length should be twice the distance as measured from your child's shoulder to her waist. Following illustration 1, cut the vest and secure the appropriate edges with white glue. When the glue has dried, turn the vest inside out to hide the seams.

For a sash, use a piece of contrasting material that is 6 inches wide and long enough to be wrapped around the waist at least twice and tied.

Use a triangular piece of material for a head scarf. A novelty sword and a big earring complete the costume.

This costume is another one of those outfits that can be easily made with regular clothes out of your family's wardrobe.

MATERIALS NEEDED
* White or colorful blouse
* Colorful full skirt
* Strings of beads (or necklaces)
* A square piece of black lace (or a silk shawl)
* Bracelets
* White glue
* Ribbon (1 inch wide)
* Earrings
* Bandanna or striped kerchief
* A long piece of colorful material 6 inches wide
* Boots (If available)

Almost any colored blouse will do. The skirt must be full. Since Hollywood has portrayed gypsies as flashy dressers, we will do likewise. Have your child wear lots of jewelry such as numerous bracelets, necklaces, strings of beads and earrings.

To give a solid colored skirt a theatrical look, glue several pieces of 1-inch ribbon horizontally around the skirt. For a sash, use a piece of red material 6 inches wide and long enough to be wrapped around the waist twice and tied. A bandanna or kerchief should be worn as a head scarf. For the final touches, place a large square of black lace over the shoulders for a shawl and if available, wear boots.

The young fortuneteller is now ready to predict the future by reading palms. When someone asks to have his palm read, use a concealed red crayon or marker to put a red dot on his palm.

Wonderful for its simplicity, the prisoner costume never fails to prove its worth for getting a laugh.

MATERIALS NEEDED
* White pajamas
* 2-inch-wide masking tape
* Black spray paint
* White painter's cap
* Plastic chain and balloon

This is an easy costume to make. Take a pair of white pajamas and remove the breast pocket. If you can't find white pajamas, beige or light blue will also suffice. Lay the pants and top on a flat surface and stripe them horizontally with 2-inch-wide masking tape. Be sure to firmly press the masking tape to the pajamas. Next, paint the pajamas with black spray paint. After the paint has dried, remove the tape. You will now have a striped pair of pants and a shirt. Stencil a serial number on the back of the costume.

Remove the brim from a white painter's cap and stripe to make a prisoner's hat. For make-up, rub a burned cork over the face to create beard stubble. A plastic ball and chain, found in most costume shops or novelty stores, makes a wonderful prop. If one is not available, use a partially inflated balloon, painted black and tied to a piece of plastic chain.

The word "Mexico" conjures up visions of friendly people, spicy food and bright colors. To take an imaginative journey to that country, your costume requirements are very simple.

MATERIALS NEEDED
* White pants
* White long-sleeved shirt
* Sandals
* Straw hat
* Two different types of colorful fabric
* Eyebrow pencil

Besides white pants and shirt, sandals, and straw hat, which should be worn as shown in the photograph, this costume will require two different types of material to make a sash and a serape.

A serape is a colorful blanket that is worn over the shoulders. To make one, obtain a striped piece of material in appropriate colors. Cut to size and wear over the shoulder as shown in the photograph.

To make a sash, use a colorful material such as a red satin. The fabric should be at least 6 inches wide and long enough to wrap around your child's waist at least twice. Tie the material in a knot around the waist and let it hang down at your child's side just above his knees.

If a mustache is desired, pencil one in with an eyebrow pencil.

HAREM GIRL

189

his costume provides the perfect companion to the sheik.

MATERIALS NEEDED

* Bikini bathing suit or dance briefs and small piece
of gold lamé
* Sheer material (such as chiffon)
* Assorted jewelry
* White glue
* Slippers

Start with a bikini bathing suit. To transform the bathing suit into a costume, take two rectangular pieces of sheer material long enough to reach from the waist to the floor. Pin one piece to the front of the briefs and the other to the back. Add beads, pearls, small chains and necklaces to trim around the waist of the skirt.

(1-A)

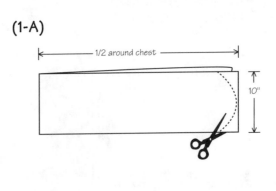

(1-B)

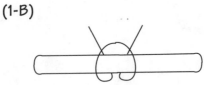

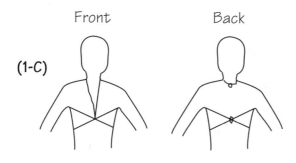

Front   Back

(1-C)

If you don't have an appropriate bathing suit, use a pair of dance briefs and make a bra out of gold lamé using the following directions. Cut a strip of material that is approximately 10 inches wide and long enough to wrap around your child's chest and tie in the back. Fold the material lengthwise in half, and with a pair of scissors, cut the ends of the material as shown in illustration 1-A. Loop a piece of cord in the center of the material as shown in illustration 1-B. Tie the free ends of the cord around the child's neck and the ends of the strips of material around her back to form a bra. (Illustration 1-C)

(2)

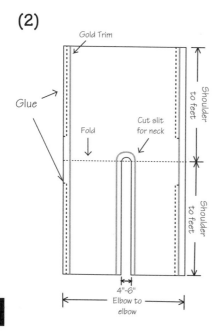

Gold Trim

Glue

Fold

Cut slit for neck

Shoulder to feet

Shoulder to feet

4"-6"
Elbow to elbow

Use a piece of sheer material as a veil or headpiece by merely bobby pinning it into the hair.

Next, you will need to make a caftan, which is an over-robe, out of the sheer material. Measure the distance from your child's shoulder to her feet. Whatever the measurement is, double it to get the length of material you will need to make the caftan. Have your child stand with her arms out from her sides like a scarecrow. Measure from elbow to elbow to get the width of material you will need to make the caftan.

Using illustration 2 as a guide, cut out a 4- to 6-inch section halfway up the center for a center front opening. The top should be rounded to fit about the neck. Glue gold trim along the sides and around the center front opening. When this is done, fold in half lengthwise and glue the sides shut leaving an opening to put the arms through.

SHEIK

With sunglasses, trousers and dress shoes, this costume can be used as a wealthy Arab sheik. Or with sandals, it can double as Lawrence of Arabia.

MATERIALS NEEDED
* White material
* Black material
* White glue
* Sandals
* Eight black or red pom-poms
* Black elastic
* Gold metallic ribbon
* Black spray paint
* 1 yard of plastic tubing

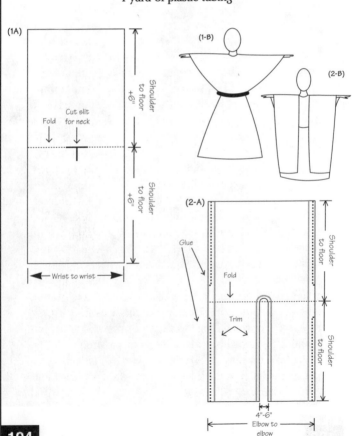

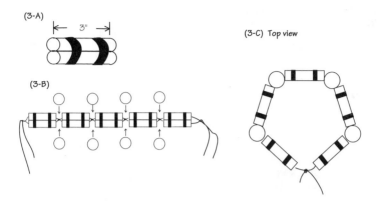

(3-A)

|← 3" →|

(3-C) Top view

(3-B)

Use white material to make the sheik's under-robe, which is essentially a very full poncho. Measure the distance from your child's shoulder to his feet. Whatever the measurement is, double it and add 12 inches to get the length of material you will need to make the under-robe. (Illustration 1-A) Next, have your child stand with his arms out from his sides like a scarecrow. Measure from wrist to wrist to get the width of material you will need to make the under-robe. With the material already folded in half lengthwise, cut a slit in the center just large enough to fit the head. This is worn like a poncho but belted in at the waist with a black sash. (Illustration 1-B) Any extra material in length is bloused up over the sash.

Next, you need to make a caftan which will be a black over-robe. Measure the distance from your child's shoulders to his feet. Whatever the measurement is, double it to have enough material for the caftan. Next, have your child stand with his arms out from his sides like a scarecrow. Measure from elbow to elbow to get the width of material you will need to make the caftan. Using illustration 2-A as a guide, cut out a 4- to 6-inch section halfway up the center for a center front opening. The top should be rounded to fit about the neck. Glue gold trim along the sides and around the center front opening. When this is done, fold in half lengthwise and glue the sides shut leaving an opening to put the arms through. (Illustration 2-B)

The Arab headpiece is the trickiest part of this costume, but if you follow our detailed instructions, you shouldn't have any problems. First you need to make the band, which you will use later to hold the cloth headpiece in place. To make this, take 1/2-inch clear plastic tubing and spray it with black spray paint. When this has dried, cut off 10 equal pieces of tubing that are about 3 inches in length. Using two pieces of tubing at a time, connect them lengthwise by gluing two bands of gold metallic ribbon 1/2 inch away from the edges. (Illustration 3-A) When you are finished, you will have five sections of double banned tubing. Connect these together by feeding in two lengths of black elastic, knotting the elastic between each section. In between the sections of tubing you must glue two pom-poms. (Illustration 3-B) When finished, tie the two free ends to finish the headband. (Illustration 3-C)

The cloth headpiece is simply a 4-foot square of soft white fabric. Place the material on your son's head with one corner underneath. (Illustration 4-A) The longest part of the cloth should be hanging down toward the center of the back. Secure the cloth to his head by slipping on the elastic headpiece. It is best to show a bit of the white fabric below the elastic band. Finally, take the right side of the cloth headpiece under the chin and place it over the left shoulder. (Illustration 4-B)

Don't forget the sandals and sunglasses. If so desired, your child could carry a plastic sword.

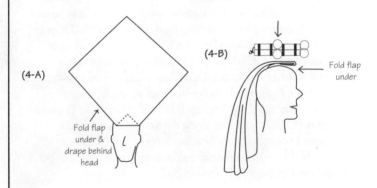

(4-A)

Fold flap under & drape behind head

(4-B)

Fold flap under

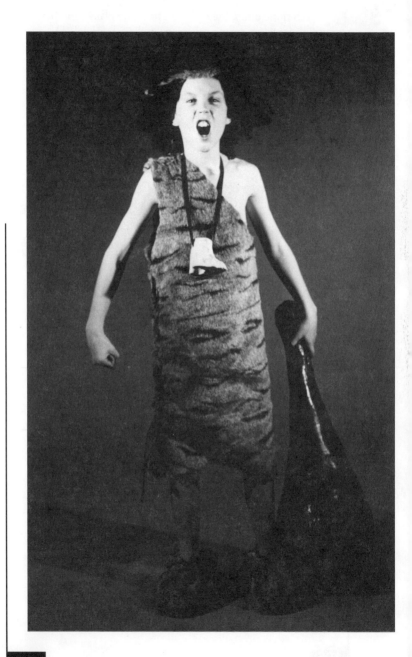

In prehistoric times, the caveman ruled the planet. But he still can be seen roaming around—in the movies, on TV and at parties.

MATERIALS NEEDED
* Fake fur material
* Rawhide or brown shoelaces
* Spare ribs
* Bleach
* Rope
* Wig
* Club

Since this costume calls for the use of fake fur, here are a few suggestions on how to cut this type of fabric. It is always best to cut fake fur from the back of the material. Instead of scissors, which cut the fibers and leave a crude edge, use a matte knife or single edge razor blade. Please use these with extreme caution.

(1-A)

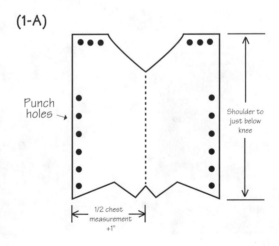

Punch holes →

Shoulder to just below knee

1/2 chest measurement +1"

(1-B)

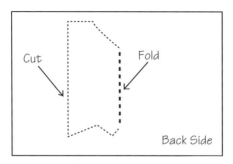

Measure the distance from your child's shoulder to just below his knee and also measure around his chest. To cut the tunic as shown in illustration 1-A, lay the material down (back side up) and sketch with chalk the front of the tunic as shown in illustration 1-B. Using a matte knife, cut all around except on the fold line. Fold the cut-out piece back along the fold line to get the pattern for the back. (Illustration 1-C) Cut out with a matte knife. Punch holes in the open sides and lace the tunic shut with rawhide or brown shoelaces.

(1-C)

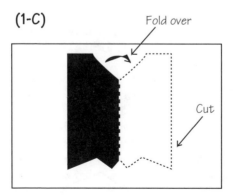

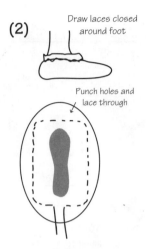

(2)

Draw laces closed around foot

Punch holes and lace through

Your son can wear his regular shoes with this outfit as long as they are disguised. To do this, use a spare piece of the fur material and follow illustration 2. Punch holes around the material and lace shut with rawhide or brown shoelaces.

If a wig is available, use one and tie a strip of fur around the head for a headband.

A spare rib necklace adds a nice theatrical touch. After the spare ribs are cleaned off, soak them in bleach to turn them white. Next, drill a hole in one end of each rib and thread them on a piece of rawhide or brown shoelace, being careful to place knots in between each rib. If you don't have spare ribs, any old bone will do.

To complete this outfit add a club. If you cannot obtain a plastic caveman's club from a costume shop or novelty store, you can make one. A club can be fashioned out of chicken wire covered with newspaper and coated entirely with white glue. The white glue will tend to soften the paper so that it takes the shape of the chicken wire. Allow the glue to dry and color the club with brown and black paint.

The whole world loves a clown, especially young children.

MATERIALS NEEDED
* Leotard and tights
* Crepe paper
* Masking tape
* Wig or funny hat
* Make-up
* Umbrella, strong black thread, ball (for clown prop)

The basic items for the clown costume are a leotard and a pair of tights. To enhance the outfit, we will add crepe paper ruffs and pom-poms.

For the neck ruff, cut a piece of crepe paper the full length of the package approximately 10 inches wide. Gather the paper to form a ruff that goes completely around your child's neck. Run a piece of masking tape through the middle of the ruff to hold the pleats in place. (Illustration 1) Use a safety pin to close about the neck.

To form ruffs for the wrists, cut two pieces of paper one-third the length of the package approximately 6 inches wide. Follow the same procedure used for the neck ruff. Pom-poms can be made out of 2-inch-wide strips of crepe paper gathered on a safety pin. Pin these to the front of the leotard and the shoes.

For make-up, outline the desired features for the eyebrows, lips, etc. with a black eyebrow pencil. (Photo 1)

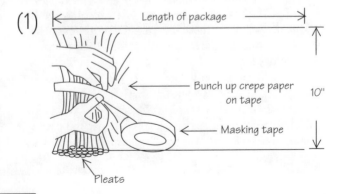

(1) Length of package

Bunch up crepe paper on tape

10"

Masking tape

Pleats

Using a brush or a (2)
sponge, apply an
even coat of clown
white to the areas of
the face that will *not* be
colored in red or black.
Come as close to the outline
as possible without touching it.
(Photo 2) Fill in the eyebrows
with black make-up. Trace
around the outer edge with the
black eyebrow pencil, filling in
between the black and white, and
leaving a neat clean line. Fill in the lips
with red make-up, coming as close to the inside of the
outline as possible. Using the black eyebrow pencil, fill in
between the white on the face and the red on the lips,
making certain the lines are sharp and clean. (Photo 3) If
grease paint make-up is used, the entire face must be
powdered. Use a soft brush to remove the excess powder.

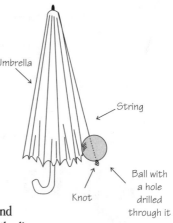

A rubber ball or novelty clown nose may be purchased
from your local costume shop. If necessary, attach the false
nose with a piece of thin white elastic. Add a brightly
colored novelty wig. Either buy one or take an old wig,
brush it out, and spray it with bright colored hair spray. Top
off your outfit with a funny looking hat.

To make a clown prop, use a regular umbrella (or
better yet, a Chinese parasol), a piece of strong black thread
and a ball. Tie one end of the thread to the tip of the center
pole of the umbrella. Attach the ball to the other end of the
string. This can be done by punching a hole through the
center of the ball and running the thread through the ball,
knotting it in place. (Illustration 2) The gag is to toss the
ball into the air while opening the umbrella. If timed
properly, it looks as if you are able to catch and balance the
ball on the edge of the spinning umbrella. After you have
amazed your audience, take your bow exposing the trick for
an extra laugh.

PHOTO #1

PHOTO #2

PHOTO #3

PHOTO #4

Howdy, partner. For kids who love cowboy movies, this outfit will help them relive the memories of the old Wild West.

MATERIALS NEEDED
* Flannel shirt
* Jeans
* Black fake fur (for chaps)
* Leather belt
* Black vinyl (for vest)
* Black shoelaces
* Hot glue gun
* Bandanna
* Cowboy hat (toy store or costume shop)

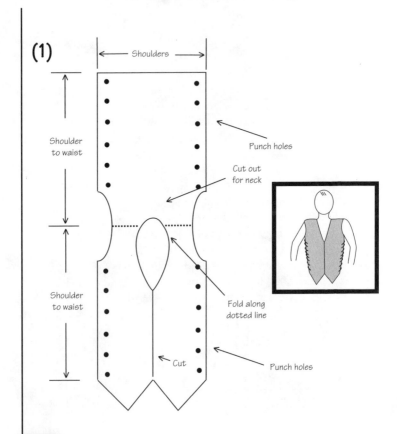

(2-A)

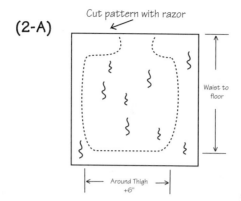

Cut pattern with razor

Waist to floor

Around Thigh
+6"

Given your son's flannel shirt and jeans, a cowboy hat bought from a toy store and a bandanna, all that remains is a vest and chaps.

A vest can be cut out of black vinyl by following illustration 1. The width of the vest should be roughly the distance between the two shoulders, while the overall length should be twice the distance as measured from your child's shoulder to just below his waist. Punch holes in the side seams and lace shut with black shoelaces.

The chaps are made from fake fur and a leather belt. It is always best to cut fake fur from the back of the material. Instead of scissors, which cut the fibers and leave a crude edge, use a matte knife or single-edge razor blade. Please use these with extreme caution. With this advice, cut two pieces of fake fur, which are mirrored images of themselves, according to illustration 2-A. Next, cut a leather belt in half and punch two holes on each of the cut ends so that these may later be laced together. (Illustration 2-B)

(2-B)

Cut & punch holes

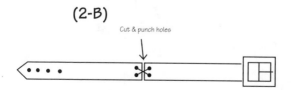

(2-C)

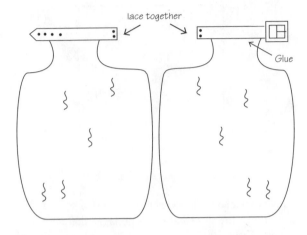

lace together

Glue

Now hot glue one piece of fur to the back of each side of the belt as shown in illustration 2-C. Lace the belt together with a shoelace. The lacing will be in the front; the chaps are worn buckled in the back. Once buckled around the waist, the chaps are pulled from the front around the legs and safety pinned in place. (Illustration 2-D)

(2-D)

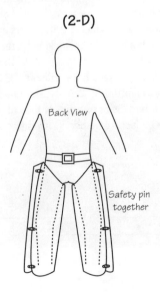

Back View

Safety pin together

VIKING BOY

Often toy, novelty and costume shops sell inexpensive viking helmets which children love to wear and make believe they are Nordic warriors. The problem for parents, come Halloween or school pageant, is how to complete the costume. If this problem ever arises, here is an easy solution.

MATERIALS NEEDED

* Non-woven, heavy material, preferably felt. Fabrics should be in rustic colors such as brown or gray.
* Fake fur
* Black, brown or gray sweat pants
* Turtleneck sweater (optional)
* Rawhide (or black or brown shoelaces)
* Plastic Viking helmet
* Plastic sword or spear
* Black vinyl (for wrist bands)

(1-A)   (1-B)

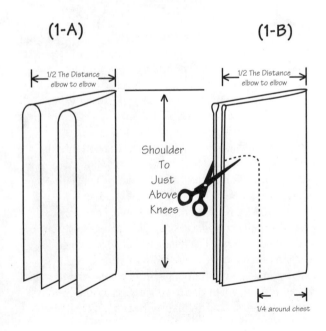

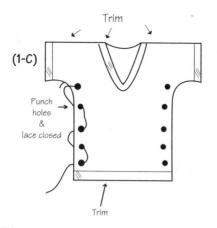

(1-C)

Trim

Punch
holes
&
lace closed

Trim

(2)

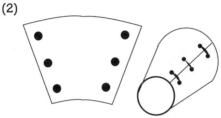

    Measure the distance from your child's shoulder to
above his knees. Whatever the measurement is, double it to
get the length of material you will need to make the tunic.
Next, have
your child stand with his arms out from his sides like a
scarecrow. Measure from elbow to elbow to get the width
of material you will need to make the tunic.
    Fold the material in half first lengthwise and then again
widthwise. (Illustration 1-A) Using illustration 1-B as a
guide, cut out the main part of the tunic. Now unfold the
material widthwise to reveal a T-shaped pattern.
(Illustration 1-C) Next, you must cut an opening for the
head. In the center front cut out a "V" large enough just to
get the head through. The tunic will fit better if you also
slightly round the back where the neck is. Enhance the
outfit by adding trim. Cut out pieces of a contrasting material
for trim and use white glue to secure it across the bottom,
around the sleeves and around the neckline. Punch holes

along the sides and lace shut with rawhide, or black or brown shoelaces.

Depending on the weather, your child might want to wear a turtleneck sweater or shirt under the tunic. Black, brown or gray sweat pants are worn for trousers. Often, sweat pants will look more rugged if they are turned inside out with the nappy material on the outside.

Following illustration 2, cut out two pieces of black vinyl that will fit comfortably around your son's wrists. Holes should be punched into each side of the vinyl and then these cuffs should be laced around your child's wrists by using either rawhide or black or brown shoelaces.

For footwear, have your son wear a pair of comfortable shoes and cover them with shoe coverings that are made by following illustration 3. Punch holes around the material and lace with rawhide or brown shoelaces. If you want to add leg wrappings, wrap strips of material around the ankle and lace around the leg, tying it off below the knee.

A Viking cape is very easy to make. Just cut an irregular shape from a fake fur and drape over the shoulders. It is always best to cut fake fur from the back of the material. Instead of scissors, which cut the fibers and leave a crude edge, use a matte knife or single edge razor blade. Please use these with extreme caution. If a broach is available, add one.

Costume shops, as wells as toy and novelty stores, often sell plastic Viking helmets, swords and spears.

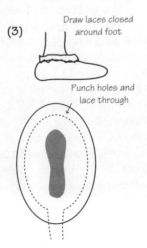

(3)

Draw laces closed around foot

Punch holes and lace through

hough the Viking girl can be a perfect companion to the Viking boy, it is just as good by itself, reminiscent of Brunhilde.

MATERIALS NEEDED
* Soft white material
* White glue
* Fancy gold cord
* Braided yellow yarn (or blonde wig)
* Plastic Viking helmet

Measure the distance from your child's shoulder to her feet. Whatever the measurement is, double it and add 12 inches to get the length of material you will need to make the robe. Next, have your child stand with her arms out from her sides like a scarecrow. Measure from wrist to wrist to get the width of material you will need to make the robe.

Fold the soft white material in half, first lengthwise and then again widthwise. (Illustration 1-A) Using scissors, cut a piece out of the lower free corners. (Illustration 1-B) Unfold the material widthwise revealing a bell-shaped pattern. (Illustration 1-C) You will now need to make an opening for the head. Cut a small slit in the center of the lengthwise

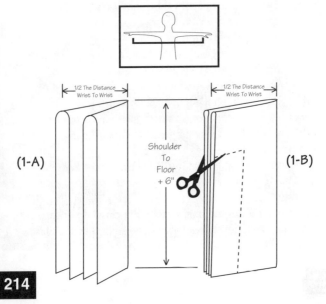

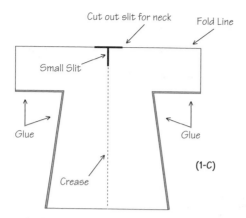

Cut out slit for neck

Fold Line

Small Slit

Glue

Glue

Crease

(1-C)

fold. Next, cut a small slit down the center front crease. Remember, it is always best not to make the openings too big. Start small and increase it gradually until your child can fit her head in easily.

Next, glue the side seams shut by applying white glue about 1/2 inch away from the edge of the fabric and then press the two pieces of material together with your fingers. When the glue has dried, turn the fabric inside out to hide the seams. The robe is belted in at the waist with a cord. Blouse any excess length over the cord. With the robe in place, crisscross a piece of fancy gold cord around the girl's chest, tying it at the waist.

You have two options for the hair. You can either braid yellow yarn into two pigtails and attach it to the helmet, or you can use a blonde wig with two plats. If the helmet fits perfectly without a wig, the first option is necessary. If the helmet is too large, try a wig. Wrap gold braid around the bottom of the plats. Using the same gold braid, make bracelets.

A plastic Viking helmet, available from most costume shops, and toy and novelty stores, is necessary to complete the costume.

If a spear is desired, make one out a closet dowel and cardboard. The spear should always be taller than the child.

JUDGE

ere comes the judge, a very effective and easy costume to make. It also makes a good companion costume for the prisoner.

MATERIALS NEEDED
* Black felt
* White felt
* Hot glue gun
* White glue
* White shirt
* White painter's cap
* White index cards

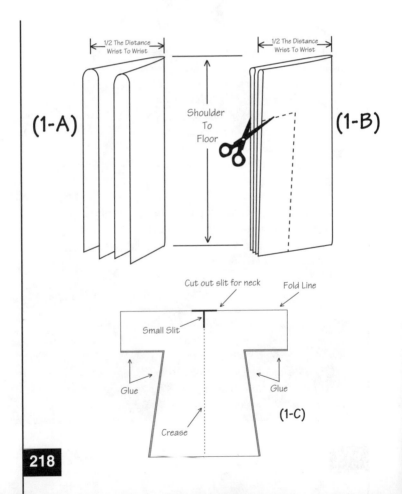

(2)

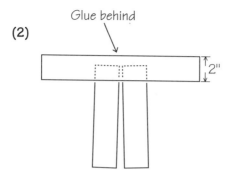

Glue behind

2"

Measure the distance from your child's shoulder to his feet. Whatever the measurement is, double it to get the length of material you will need to make the robe. Next, have your child stand with his arms out from his sides like a scarecrow. Measure from wrist to wrist to get the width of material you will need to make the robe.

Fold the material in half, first lengthwise and then again widthwise. (Illustration 1-A) Cut a piece out of the lower free corners as shown in illustration 1-B. Unfold the material widthwise revealing a bell-shaped pattern. (Illustration 1-C) Make an opening for the head by cutting a slit in the center lengthwise fold. Also make a slit down the center front crease. It is always best not to make the openings too big. Start small and increase it gradually until your child can fit his head in easily. Glue the side seams shut by applying white glue about 1/2 inch away from the edge of the fabric and then press the two pieces of material together with your fingers. When the glue has dried, turn the robe inside out to hide the seams.

Next, you need to make a white judge's collar. Using white felt, cut out three 2-inch strips of material. One piece will be safety pinned around the neck while the other two pieces will either be glued or pinned to the front of the collar so that they hang downwards, as shown in illustration 2. It is best to wear a white shirt underneath the over-robe.

A judge's wig can be made as follows. Start by cutting off the brim of a white painter's cap. (Illustration 3-A) Next, cut six strips of white felt measuring about 12 inches long by 3 inches wide. Hot glue two strips to the back of the hat and two strips on both sides of the cap. (Illustration 3-B) Next create the illusion of white curls of hair by taking white index cards and rolling and gluing them into tubes. Starting at the bottom of each felt strip, hot glue the paper rolls. (Illustration 3-C) Continue this process working up the six felt strips, and continue up until the entire painter's cap is covered. (Illustration 3-D)

Once the wig and robe are done, the court is now in session, so would everyone please rise and have some fun.

(3-A)

(3-B)

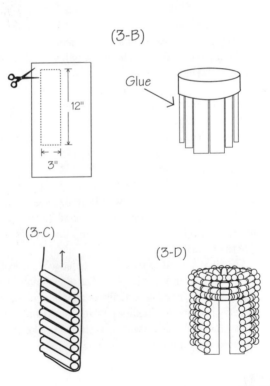

Glue

(3-C)

(3-D)

his is a very easy costume to put together and is perfect for summer pool parties.

MATERIALS NEEDED
* Bright floral pattern material
* Plastic or real flower
* Lei

Cut a strip of material that is approximately 10 inches wide and long enough to wrap around your child's chest and tie in the back. Fold the material lengthwise in half and, with a pair of scissors, cut the ends of the material as shown in illustration 1-A. Loop a piece of cord in the center of the material as shown in illustration 1-B. Tie the free ends of the cord around the child's neck and the ends of the strips of material around her back to form a bra. (Illustration 1-C)

(1-A)

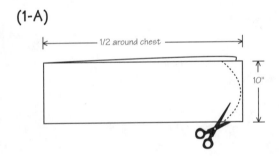

(1-B)

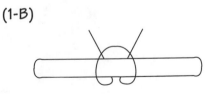

(1-C)

Front   Back

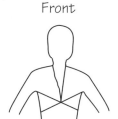

(2)

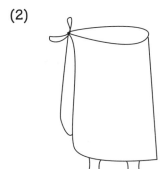

Using the same material, make a sarong. A sarong is simply a rectangular piece of material. The width is long enough to be wrapped around and tied about the waist, and the length should be from your child's waist to below her knees. (Illustration 2)

To spice up the costume, add a flower in the hair and a lei, obtainable from most costume shops or novelty stores.

The jester was a clown who was retained by royalty to provide casual entertainment in the courts of kings and queens.

MATERIALS NEEDED
* Leotard and tights (In colors such as red or yellow)
* Red and yellow felt
* White glue
* Fancy gold cord
* White crepe paper
* Masking tape
* Ballet slippers
* Make-up
* Baby doll's head, dowel and ribbons (for the bauble)

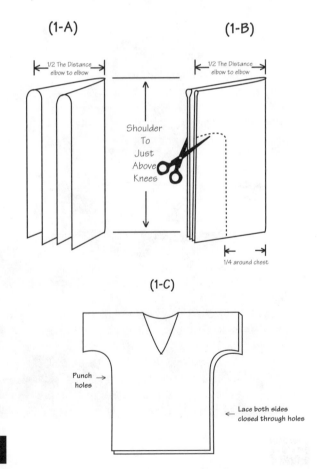

226

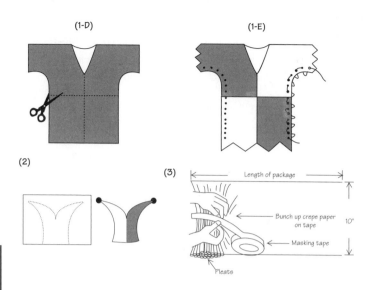

(1-D)   (1-E)

(2)   (3)

Length of package

Bunch up crepe paper
on tape

Masking tape

10"

Pleats

The jester's costume has many color combinations from
which to choose; black and white, green and red, yellow
and red, etc. Our personal favorite is yellow and red. The
basic parts of the jester's costume is a leotard and a pair of
tights. You may wish to use a red leotard and tights, or a
yellow leotard and tights, or even mix and match the sets.
It is purely your choice.

In addition to the leotard and tights, you will also need
to make a tunic. Measure the distance from your child's
shoulder to right above his knees. Whatever the measurement
is, double it to get the length of material you will need to
make the tunic. Have your child stand with his arms straight
out from his sides like a scarecrow. Measure from elbow to
elbow to get the width of material you will need to make
the tunic.

Fold a piece of yellow material in half first lengthwise
and then again widthwise. (Illustration 1-A) Using
illustration 1-B as a guide, cut out the main part of the tunic.
Now unfold the material widthwise to reveal a T-shaped
pattern. (Illustration 1-C) Using this piece as a pattern, cut
out a second piece of felt in a contrasting color such as red.
Cut this piece in quarters as shown in illustration 1-D. With

white glue, glue one quarter of the red felt to the upper left front of the yellow tunic and one quarter to the lower right. Glue the other two quarters to the opposite sides on the back of the tunic. When the glue has dried, cut an opening for the head. (Illustration 1-E) In the center front cut out a "V" large enough just to get the head through. The tunic will fit better if you also slightly round the hole at the back where the neck is. To help give the outfit a comical look jag the edges as shown in the diagram. If you like, pin small bells, pom-poms or tassels to the ends of the jags. The tunic can be held together by punching holes along the sides and lacing it shut with gold cord.

To make the hat, use a piece of yellow felt and follow illustration 2. Apply white glue about 1/2 inch away from the edge of the fabric and then press the two pieces of material together with your fingers. Make an identical pattern out of one piece of red felt. Cut the material directly in the center and, with white glue, glue one half to the front of the hat and the other half on the opposite side on the back. For added decoration, pin small bells, pom-poms or tassels to the ends of the hat.

To assemble, put on the leotard and tights and then the ballet slippers. Next, slip on the tunic and draw it closer to your child's waist with a piece of gold cord. For a neck ruff, cut a piece of white crepe paper the full length of the package approximately 10 inches wide. Gather the paper to form a ruff that goes completely around your child's neck. Use a strip of masking tape through the middle of the ruff to hold the pleats in place. Safety pin the ruff around the neck. (Illustration 3)

Black, white and red are standard colors for a jester's make-up. The following photographs may prove to be a guide on how the make-up should be applied. When the make-up application is complete, don the jester's hat.

A bauble, a doll-like replica of oneself, makes a wonderful prop piece. By using some leftover felt, some ribbons, a few pom-poms, a wooden dowel and a small baby doll's head, the bauble should be relatively easy to make if you follow the photographs on the next page.

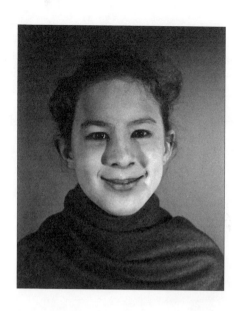

All COOL HAND titles are available through your local bookstore or by mail. To order directly, return the coupon below to: COOL HAND COMMUNICATIONS, INC., Order Department, 1098 N.W. Boca Raton Blvd., Boca Raton, FL 33432.

New for 1993 (COOL HAND Creations)

Quantity

How to Cope With Chronic Pain	1-56790-043-7	$9.95
National Park Vacations: The West-Vol. 1	1-56790-012-7	$9.95
Creative Costumes for Children	1-56790-059-3	$11.95
Life & Love in the Paradise Lounge	1-56790-115-8	$6.95
Unfinished Business	1-56790-000-3	$22.95

Lynn Allison Better Lifestyle Series:

1001 Ways/Life Better	1-56790-097-6	$7.95
The Magic of Garlic	1-56790-098-4	$7.95
Natural Stress-Busters	1-56790-099-2	$7.95
Uncommon Footsteps	1-56790-149-2	$19.95
Hit of the Party	1-56790-063-1	$14.95
World's Worst Cookbook	1-56790-137-9	$8.95

Backlist Beauties (COOL HAND Classics)

Think A Little	1-56790-025-9	$7.95
Compleat Option Player	0-89709-200-7	$14.95
Creative Costumes	1-56790-056-9	$6.95
Dr. Cookie's Cookbook (Comb)	1-56790-109-3	$7.95
Dr. Cookie's Cookbook (Paper)	1-56790-108-5	$6.95
Early American Cookbook	1-56790-087-9	$7.95
Essential Book of Shellfish	1-56790-125-5	$6.95
How to Be a Wine Expert	1-9613525-1-5	$9.95
Muffin Mania	1-56790-074-7	$7.95
One Day Celestial Navigation	1-56790-021-6	$9.95

Sub-total _____

Please add $2.00 for postage and handling. _____

Florida residents add 6.5% sales tax to order. _____

TOTAL _____

Bill To: _____

_____

_____

_____

Ship To: _____

_____

_____

_____